Northern Windows/Southern Stars

Reimagining Ireland

Volume 109

Edited by Dr Eamon Maher,
Technological University Dublin – Tallaght Campus

PETER LANG
Oxford • Bern • Berlin • Bruxelles • New York • Wien

Northern Windows/ Southern Stars

Selected Early Essays 1983–1994

Gerald Dawe

PETER LANG

Oxford • Bern • Berlin • Bruxelles • New York • Wien

Bibliographic information published by Die Deutsche Nationalbibliothek. Die Deutsche Nationalbibliothek lists this publication in the Deutsche Nationalbibliografie; detailed bibliographic data is available on the Internet at http://dnb.d-nb.de.

A catalogue record for this book is available from the British Library.

Library of Congress Cataloging-in-Publication Data

Names: Dawe, Gerald, 1952- author.
Title: Northern windows/southern stars : selected early essays 1983-1994 / Gerald Dawe.
Description: Oxford ; New York : Peter Lang, 2022. | Series: Reimagining Ireland, 16629094 ; vol no.109 | Includes bibliographical references.
Identifiers: LCCN 2021059764 (print) | LCCN 2021059765 (ebook) | ISBN 9781800796522 (paperback) | ISBN 9781800796539 (ebook) | ISBN 9781800796546 (epub)
Subjects: LCGFT: Essays.
Classification: LCC PR6054.A915 N67 2022 (print) | LCC PR6054.A915 (ebook) | DDC 824/.914--dc23/eng/20211213
LC record available at https://lccn.loc.gov/2021059764
LC ebook record available at https://lccn.loc.gov/2021059765

Cover image: Harry Aaron Kernoff (1900–1974), *Geometric Star Pattern in Sphere*, Watercolour, ink and graphite on paper, 8.5 cm.
NGI.7766.34, National Gallery of Ireland Collection. Photo © National Gallery of Ireland © The Artist's Estate.
Cover design by Peter Lang Ltd.

ISSN 1662-9094
ISBN 978-1-80079-652-2 (print)
ISBN 978-1-80079-653-9 (ePDF)
ISBN 978-1-80079-654-6 (ePub)

© Peter Lang Group AG 2022

Published by Peter Lang Ltd, International Academic Publishers, 52 St Giles, Oxford, OX1 3LU, United Kingdom oxford@peterlang.com, www.peterlang.com

Gerald Dawe has asserted his right under the Copyright, Designs and Patents Act, 1988, to be identified as Author of this Work.

All rights reserved.
All parts of this publication are protected by copyright.
Any utilisation outside the strict limits of the copyright law,
without the permission of the publisher, is forbidden and liable to prosecution.
This applies in particular to reproductions, translations, microfilming,
and storage and processing in electronic retrieval systems.

This publication has been peer reviewed.

For all students of poetry
And in memory of Dennis O'Driscoll

Contents

Preface ix

Acknowledgements xiii

CHAPTER 1
Brief Confrontations 1

CHAPTER 2
A Gritty Prod Baroque: Tom Paulin 13

CHAPTER 3
Northern Windows/Southern Stars 31

CHAPTER 4
A Question of Imagination 43

CHAPTER 5
How's the Poetry Going? 55

CHAPTER 6
Invocation of Powers: John Montague 65

CHAPTER 7
Potent Music: Yeats's Legacy 83

CHAPTER 8
Critical Mass 93

CHAPTER 9
The Parochial Idyll: W. R. Rodgers   103

CHAPTER 10
An Unmoved Mind: John Millington Synge   111

CHAPTER 11
Our Secret Being: Padraic Fiacc   121

CHAPTER 12
Breathing Spaces: Brendan Kennelly   131

NICHOLAS ALLEN
Afterword   139

Bibliography   149

Preface

Looking back to when these essays were first written is chastening. For a start it is difficult to imagine how things were in the 1980s and early 1990s in an Ireland, north and south, still trying to adjust to the ongoing tragic impact of the Troubles, the slowly dawning public realization of the extent of human travesty conducted in the name of the Catholic Church (in the main) and the realignments which were taking place in our economic and political engagements with Britain and Europe. In what would become the defining symbolic act of the period – the election of Mary Robinson to the presidency of Ireland in 1990 – the surrounding literary and cultural conditions in the country were also changing as decades of economic policies ran into the ground and emigration soared. What had been a profoundly conservative society on both sides of the border, started to unwind. Now, half a century after the earliest of these essays first appeared, it is disorientating for me as writer and, I suspect, for the reader as well, to recognize how much actually *has* changed and how quickly. When we bear in mind the impact of Brexit and, hot on its angry heels, the Covid-19 pandemic with its terrible loss of life, the moral and ideological disaster of 'Trumpism', the world of twenty-first-century Ireland is indeed a very different place.

These though are factors well beyond the scope and competence of the present writer. Safe to say, however, that inscribed in this gathering of essays, devoted to writing from Ireland, there is, I hope, a justified and validated conviction that poetry matters. While the pressing issues today which swirl around the making and reading of poetry – of which gender equality, diversity, and inclusivity are the most currently debated – it is important to say that these issues are in themselves historical and form part of a longer and wider narrative of Irish, British, and North American cultural history. These essays only touch upon such matters tangentially since their concerns at the time of writing were other, generally trying to draw attention to lesser-known (male) poets whose work was being re-issued, such as W. R. Rodgers or Padraic Fiacc. An early essay on Eavan Boland's poetry collections, including *The War Horse* and *Night Feed*, along with other literary essays and editorial work will appear in a forthcoming collection, *Politic Words: Essays in Irish Women's Writing 1985–2022*.

Some of the aesthetic concerns raised in *Northern Windows/Southern Stars* such as the influence of critical judgement and debate on how Irish writing, and in particular poetry, was viewed during the 1980s and early 1990s, seems now to belong to a literary culture that is no longer widely shared but is, on the contrary, dismissed as 'elitist'. With the opportunities provided by online publication and the volume of material published online, in blogs, in digital magazines – and increasingly performed as spoken verse, in Rap-like sessions, Open Mic, in festivals throughout the country – it was only a matter of time before the idea of 'criticism' itself would become identified in the media and in the academy as an exclusionist act of forlorn patriarchal gate-keepers, even if judgements were often most trenchantly made by women critics.

Re-reading these essays in the 2020s will seem for many, I have little doubt, to be an exercise in historical re-visitation; going back, that is, to how things appeared to one who was trying to reason equably with himself and a relatively small, yet engaged readership of 'little' magazines in Ireland and elsewhere. The questions raised were about what was 'good' in this poet or that verse; about what was happening inside the culture as the forces of politics, or the rising influence of various cultural forces – marketing, PR, and the proliferation of literature as entertainment – became increasingly more popular in Irish society from the late 1980s and 1990s onwards. The work included here was mostly based on personal impression, and the tentative conclusions reached in, say, 'Critical Mass', were not meant to be anything more than that – impressions, soundings, shots in the dark. Most of what follows was written in the spaces between a fairly demanding teaching schedule and the needs of finding the time and sympathetic routine for producing poems of my own. What connects these different factors was the students, to whom this book is dedicated – along with the late and much missed poet-critic Dennis O'Driscoll – students of poetry who for forty years or so matched and superseded my love of the art with their own ideas, experience, and knowledge in lecture hall, seminar room and tutorial office. It was never really a job, or a 'career'. If I led the conversation, they, from all various arts and parts of Ireland, the UK, Europe, US, and further afield, took over and made it, to quote Philip Larkin's poem 'The Trees', 'afresh, afresh, afresh'.

– Gerald Dawe
Dún Laoghaire
County Dublin
December 2021

Acknowledgements

Northern Windows/Southern Stars is a selection of the poetry and literary essays which were originally collected in *The Proper Word: Ireland, Poetry, Politics*, edited with an introduction by Nicholas Allen and published by David Gardiner in the United States in 2007. A revised and shortened version of Professor Allen's introduction to that volume is included here with his consent as a retrospective. I want to thank Jonathan Williams for all his help over many decades; his contribution to the wider Irish literary scene has been indispensable; and to the fine scholar Conor Linnie who brought the diverse material into working order, good wishes and thanks for his patience. With the publisher I would like to acknowledge the following books, journals, and magazines where the material in *Northern Windows/Southern Stars* was originally published along with the editors and publishers who commissioned the essays identified below in chronological order of their publication date:

'Brief Confrontations: The Irish Writer's History', *The Crane Bag* Vol. 7, No. 2, 1983.

'A Gritty Prod Baroque: Tom Paulin', *Irish Literary Supplement* Vol. 3. No. 1, 1984, *Honest Ulsterman* No. 82, Winter 1986 and No. 84, Winter 1987, *The Irish Times*, 16 November 1996.

'Northern Windows/Southern Stars', *Linen Hall Review,* Winter 1987, Spring 1988, Spring 1989.

'A Question of Imagination', *Cultural Contexts and Literary Idioms in Contemporary Irish Literature*, edited by Michael Kenneally. Gerrard's Cross: Colin Smythe, 1988.

'How's the Poetry Going?' *Rhinoceros* Magazine, Autumn, 1990.

'Invocation of Powers: John Montague', *The Chosen Ground: Essays on Contemporary Poetry from Northern Ireland*, edited by Neil Corcoran. Mid-Glamorgan: Seren Books, 1992.

'Critical Mass: Poetry and Ireland in the 1980s', *The Linen Hall Review*, Autumn, 1993.

'Potent Music', An Introduction, *Yeats: a new selection*, edited by Gerald Dawe. Dublin: Anna Livia Press, 1993.

'The Parochial Idyll: W. R. Rodgers', *Honest Ulsterman*, No. 92, 1993.

'An Unmoved Mind: J M Synge' was written for an edition of Synge's poetry which was unpublished. 1994.

'Our Secret Being: Padraic Fiacc', *Ruined Pages: Selected Poems of Padraic Fiacc*, edited by Gerald Dawe and Aodán Mac Póilin. Belfast: Blackstaff Press, 1994.

'Breathing Spaces: Brendan Kennelly', *Dark Fathers into Light: Brendan Kennelly*, edited by Richard Pine. Newcastle-upon-Tyne: Bloodaxe Books, 1994.

CHAPTER 1

Brief Confrontations

In his 1966 address to the Modern Language Association in New York, Thomas Kinsella remarked:

> ... for the present – especially in this present – it seems that every writer has to make the imaginative grasp at identity for himself; and if he can find no means in his inheritance to suit him, he will have to start from scratch.[1]

The assumption that the writer is constitutionally free to 'start from scratch', that there are no ineradicable blemishes or scars, might appear too idealistic. It marks, however, an important demarcation in the deterministic vocabularies of 'influence', 'roots', and 'place' that occupy so much of the discussion about the nature of Irish poetry in the English language. The freedom, the *necessary* freedom Kinsella suggests, is for the writer to choose his or her imaginative identity and, if that identity is framed by an inappropriate tradition, then it is the writer's responsibility to create an alternative tradition that liberates.

It is an awkward point summoning up those perpetual questions: to what extent is the writer truly free to create his or her own tradition? How does a writer's own identity 'fit' into a tradition? What is a tradition – a home, a prison, a cave?

It seems to me that Kinsella answers these questions for himself in the 1966 address, leaving the theoretical matter unresolved while, simultaneously, clearing the cluttered places of Irish history and myth to make space for his own creativity.

The questions re-emerge, however, when we consider the finished products of such creative moments: have they engaged things and places

---

[1] Thomas Kinsella, 'The Irish Writer,' in *Davis, Mangan, Ferguson? Tradition and the Irish Writer* (Dublin: Dolmen Press, 1970), 66.

outside of themselves? Immediately we are back in the treacherous seas of what literature is, what it means, and how we can evaluate it.

I do not intend to tackle here any of these issues directly but rather to consider the abstract creative moment and to define a few of the levers of power that are, to my mind, exerted upon it by what Thomas Kinsella calls 'inheritance'. My concern is with process, the transformation that takes place on interacting levels between the past (as inheritance) and the present (as creative moment), and the expressive form this activity establishes as a literary convention.

Transformations, processes, and changes are most difficult to define, presupposing a clear-sighted point at which we can identify something as it alters, modifies itself, and becomes different. 'Dates' are signposts marking shifts and movements, imperceptible or overt, but rarely adequate to the complexity of what happened or is in the process of becoming.

It seems as if we are dumb before the Chinese box of history or that we must applaud Madame Guillotine as she rigidly exacts her meaning. Either way, we look like acquiescent adepts of hindsight willing to accept what the past is with a troubled conscience that it is the 'Past', bearing down upon us in controllably subterranean ways while remaining, paradoxically, petrified. It is only when the past erupts in the present that it becomes more than rhetorical; its meaning is no longer assumed.

This paradox, which on a social level means conflict, exists as a lever of power in what I have vaguely called the creative moment, the present. Denis Donoghue alluded to the problem when he wrote:

> ... it is my impression that Irish writers sense a rift between experience and meaning, but in reverse; the meaning is premature, already inscribed by a mythology they have no choice but to inherit, and the experience is too narrow to be entirely natural and representative.[2]

One can itemize this rift by referring to the terms that are generally used to describe 'Irish experience' but are shied away from on an intellectual level: Protestant/Catholic, worker/owner, and male/female. Around

---

2   Denis Donoghue, 'Being Irish Together,' *The Sewanee Review*, Vol. LXXXIV, No. 1 (Winter 1976), 133.

these terms lie the experiences and mythologies out of which the writer works, imaginatively transcending, one hopes, their intransigent contradiction, but not reducing them either to sociological ascriptions or exploiting them merely in the interest of local colour. By referring to these terms, I do not want to prosecute a case for what is or is not 'relevant'. On the contrary, it is the claims of such terms, the ways in which they insidiously or oppressively govern the self, that need analysis. This can be achieved most permanently through works of the imagination. Yet there are several aspects of modern Irish poetry that suggest that such an analysis is resisted, that the literary tradition actively consorts *against* definition by promoting instead abstract strategies about 'the national identity', or more recently, 'regionalism', amongst other agendas.

Take, for example, a poem such as F. R. Higgins's much anthologized 'Father and Son'. In the guise of a consciously naïve language, the poem is contained within a fixed framework of response:

> Yes, happy in Meath with me for a day
> He walked, taking stock of herds in their own breathing;
> And naming colts, gusty as the wind, once steered by his hand,
> Lightnings winked in the eyes that were half shy in greeting
> Old friends; the wild blades, when he gallivanted the land.

What distinguishes this passage, with its stylized voice ('Yes, happy in Meath'), the inclusive metaphor ('colts, gusty as the wind'), the colloquialism ('gallivanted'), and the assumption of a compliant audience from, say, Padraic Colum's 'Plougher' is the latter's muscular Whitmanesque exhortation:

> Sunset and silence! A man; around him earth savage, earth broken;
> Beside him two horses, a plough!

Rather than explore a vernacular – the language we speak in – both these poems formalize its literary use. The poet's acceptance of a convention that involves recurrent images and stock motifs means that the poem 'writes itself'. This form of 'literary language', as an inheritance, generally has been related to the rural bases of Irish history and mythology.

Irish poetry's dependence upon Nature as a source of metaphor has often been remarked upon.³ Taken on a parallel level, one can see that much of modern Irish poetry has been descriptive, passively registering this dominant convention. As Michael D. Higgins has written, in another context:

> ... that writing which has drawn the most public attention has unfailingly been informed by nostalgia, or on occasion its variation, bitter memory. To jog the sensibilities into a critical self-appraisal has been dangerous at least.⁴

The critical self-appraisal referred to here has been obscured precisely because of the dominant poetic convention represented by figures such as Padraic Colum and F. R. Higgins. We can take this point one step further by considering the belief in a native Irish legacy whereby language itself is viewed as inherently 'poetical' and its stock of images an open medium for rendering meaning. The poet merely dips in and draws forth 'poetry'. In Ireland, it seems, we have accepted this notion of a 'poetic language' and have consequently neglected the critical faculty. We have also accepted, by implication at least, a certain way of looking at the world as an infallible ordinance of predictability. The self is insufficient, so moral and political responsibilities are assumed by those who 'know better' and who, with this knowledge converted into power, control our world. The poetic language, the belief in such a thing, is a language of myth, sanctities, and obligative truths, and it colludes with the conventionalized history of significant events: 1690, 1848, 1916.⁵ The meaning, as Denis Donoghue remarked, is premature; it is given, institutionalized, deterministic. The creative moment, the present, is swept aside, inundated with one version of the past, and with it the complex relationship of the self with the world it inhabits is trivialized. It is this relationship that Thomas Kinsella

---

3   See, for instance, Seamus Heaney's 'The Sense of Place,' *Preoccupations: Selected Prose 1968–1978* (London: Faber & Faber, 1980).
4   M. D. Higgins, 'Liam O'Flaherty and Peadar O'Donnell: Images of Rural Community? The Location of Some Issues in the Sociology of Literature,' paper read at the University of Hull, 1977. See *The Crane Bag*, Vol. 9, No. 1, 1985, 41–48.
5   Hannah Arendt, 'Introduction: Walter Benjamin 1892–1940' in Walter Benjamin's *Illuminations: Essays and Reflections* (London: Cape, 1970), 40.

is referring to in the opening quotation, a relationship that he seeks in his own work to explicate, protect, and be free.

It would, of course, be foolish to assume that Higgins or Colum were consciously spokespeople for a dominant literary convention. It was, after all, Yeats who propagated that convention in modern Ireland. Yet he was master of it and this mastery was sustained by the peculiar power his imagination derived from the idea of an alternative tradition, one that he had 'built from scratch'.[6]

The idea of the 'noble and beggarman' enabled Yeats to dramatize conflicting sets of metaphors and their associated emotional, cultural, and political states. The idea was, as Seamus Deane has shown, historical fiction.[7] John Hewitt formed an alternative tradition too, less spectacular than Yeats's, but one substantiated by Hewitt's meticulous historical retrieval of the Rhyming Weavers and their submerged artisan culture.[8]

It is significant that these poets (Yeats and Hewitt) are Protestant (and I am using the terms 'Protestant' and 'Catholic' in the sense that they distinguish the access a writer may or may not have in Ireland to mythic and symbolic realities).[9] It is an access that was more limited in the Protestant tradition or, to put this another way, the Protestant tradition in Ireland seemed less compatible to the artistic imagination. Consequently, 'Protestant' writers like Yeats, Synge, Beckett, and Hewitt made the constructing of an imaginative inheritance a substantial part of their literary identity and ambition, a priority that they, as individuals but in common, began 'from scratch'.[10]

---

6   W. B. Yeats, 'The Municipal Gallery Revisited,' *Collected Poems of W. B. Yeats* (London: Macmillan, 1969), 369.

7   Seamus Deane, 'The Literary Myths of The Revival: A Case for Their Abandonment,' in *Myth and Reality in Irish Literature*, ed. Joseph Ronsley (Waterloo, Ontario: Wilfrid Laurier University Press, 1977).

8   John Hewitt, *Rhyming Weavers* (Belfast: Blackstaff Press, 1974).

9   See John Hewitt's poem 'The Scar,' where the two traditions interact as 'a chance meeting / That brief confrontation.' *The Selected John Hewitt* (Belfast: Blackstaff Press, 1981), 26.

10   The fact that a popular Protestant tradition of ballad and folk art still thrives does not undermine, I think, the specifically literary context of my argument.

Undoubtedly both traditions can be limiting and restrictive to the individual writer who has been shaped by them. My point is that the Catholic writer has had a more direct, fluent, and engaged relationship with the metaphoric and symbolic sources that cluster around the idea of an Irish poetic inheritance; to pretend otherwise glosses over important aspects of that inheritance. Thomas Kinsella's comment shows that his own scrupulous brooding on this theme anticipates a possible 'new' departure, though dated years ago in 1968.

Returning to writers such as F. R. Higgins, we can see that his relationship as a Protestant to such sources was artificially constructed, lacking the conflict Yeats found through other imaginatively fertile perspectives, such as the lure of Byzantium. Padraic Colum's poetry, on the other hand, reveals how easy it was (and still is) for a Catholic writer in Ireland to exploit the homiletic and complicit form of expression.

It is a tendency Patrick Kavanagh was to debate with himself throughout his mature writing years. His response to what he finally came to see as the debasing notion of the Yeats-inspired 'peasant quality' deprived him, for a time at least, of absorbing the aesthetic design and composure of Yeats's poetry. Indeed, Kavanagh seemed to hesitate between different images of himself as a poet.

His earlier confidence in writing was drawn from the 'natural' place the figure of the poet had held in a rural community, but through his Gibb 'the poet', Kavanagh needed to create for himself a more self-consciously literary identity. This he never consistently did, and the instability of his artistic achievements is the result.

In reacting against the discredited myth, though, Kavanagh also dismissed the poems he had written under its influence: 'The Irish audience I came into contact with tried to draw out of me everything that was loud, journalistic and untrue.'[11] In his poem 'The Hero',[12] the ironic opening conceals, one suspects, the real uncertainties, echoing back to Kavanagh's experience of literary Dublin:

---

11   Patrick Kavanagh, *Collected Pruse* (London: Martin Brian & O'Keeffe, 1973), 16.
12   Patrick Kavanagh, 'The Hero', *Come Dance with Kitty Stobling and Other Poems* (London: Longmans, 1960), 35.

> He was an ordinary man, a man full of humour,
> Born for no high sacrifice, to be no marble god;
> But all the gods had failed that harvest and someone spread
>   the rumour
> That he might be deluded into taking on the job.
> And they came to him in the spring
> And said: you are our poet-king.

Kavanagh's uncertainty about his identity as a poet was subsumed in the greater threat of illness to his life. The doubt and punishing self-consciousness remained: what was the *authentic* role and voice of the poet? How was he to strike out of such orthodoxies of a conventional 'poetic' language, and find his real voice? Kavanagh's answers were, in part, negatives; he debunked 'art' and in its place substituted the ordinary: '… to wallow in the habitual, the banal / grow with nature again as before I grew.'

We are still dealing with that particular inheritance. Yet it is instructive to consider a similar process in the work of Padraic Fiacc since he exhibits, like Kavanagh, a prejudice against the mythology of art and the poet. In Fiacc's poetry, however, the prejudice is obsessive, fed by what he sees as the disabling claims of Irish history and the dominating idioms of conventional Irish poetry. What is more, the ordinary and the commonplace are transformed in Fiacc's poetry by the bloody events of Northern Ireland's history.

Fiacc's poem 'Elegy in "The Holy Land"'[13] is a good example of his relation to the Irish past. Like many of his poems, 'Elegy …' records Fiacc's disenchantment with the political, cultural, and religious nationalism that has shaped his identity as a poet. The poem sets itself against the idolizing incantation of Mangan's 'Dark Rosaleen' with the latter's 'my Queen / My life of life, my saint of saints', her 'bright face' clouded like 'the mournful moon'. It is this woman, 'at home … in your emerald bowers', whose vision Mangan seeks to free:

> But yet … will I rear your throne
> Again in golden sheen;
> 'Tis you shall reign, shall reign alone,
> My Dark Rosaleen!

---

13 Padraic Fiacc, 'Elegy in "The Holy Land"', *Odour of Blood: Poems from Northern Ireland* (Dublin: The Goldsmith Press, 1973), 36.

As with other such poems or *aisling*, the poet proclaims, with a barely concealed identification of the woman as Ireland, the inevitable sacrifice:

> O! the Erne shall run red
> With redundance of blood,
> The earth shall rock beneath our tread,
> And flames wrap hill and wood,
> And gun-peal, and slogan cry
> Wake many a glen serene
> Ere you shall fade, ere you shall die,
> My Dark Rosaleen!

We are in the customary setting of one dominant inheritance – the blood sacrifice and the hope of eventual freedom rooted in struggle. The poem's conventional landscape underlies the reverence of its vision and is saved from maudlin sentimentality only by the forcefulness of lines like these:

> The Erne … at its highest flood,
> I dashed across unseen,
> For there was lightning in my blood,
> My Dark Rosaleen!

Fiacc's poem takes this commentary as assumed: he writes directly out of the tradition in which a poem like 'Dark Rosaleen' would have the implicit emotional resonance of an immediately recognizable nostalgia of cherished ideals. Such a tradition of what was called 'the physical force' of republicanism still exists in Ireland, despite the attempts of political or cultural 'revisionists' to disarm it. Fiacc's poem confronts it on a variety of levels. The form of 'Elegy …' is disjunctive, undermining the audience's compliance; the landscape is urban and the vision has been transmogrified to a

> Girl with the whooping cough
>   gliding
> Through the wall-tall, caved-in
> Cliffs of us being kids

The sickly child is, nevertheless, part of an inherited vision, her identity as a 'small unsmiling / self / With a doll's pram' not lost but defined by 'this / Black shame on us low / -land Scotch drunks call being alive'. The ending of the poem distils the contradiction between vision and reality, an ending that sees the vision (in its rewritten form) as a legacy drawn from the persistent conventional metaphors of the Irish past:

> O dolly-Eurydice, my dark Ros-
> aleen dream
>   of bog on bog of bone
> -grounded cloud, Ireland, my dear
>
> Dragon, seed, pod …

What Kavanagh and Fiacc have, nominally, in common is a sense of myth, inheritance, and the past crumbling in the hands of their present. They express, on different imaginative levels, the 'rift between experience and meaning', but with Fiacc this rift has become a condition of his own creativity, expressed formally in the shape and experience of the poetry itself. His has become a truly modern fragmented voice.

It seems, though, that the poetic convention that Yeats propagated was maintained by poets such as Higgins and Colum and subsequently reinvigorated by Kavanagh in his best-known poems – 'Epic', or 'Kerr's Ass', for example. Kavanagh tried, however, to redefine the convention to accord more with its own self-awareness and experience of Irish life. In style, technique, and form, Kavanagh updated the convention without actually transforming it. It continues to dominate Irish poetry.

In this reading, and given the testimony of poets such as John Montague and Seamus Heaney, Kavanagh stands as *the* most important figure in Irish poetry of the last half of the twentieth century. His presence is continuously reaffirmed in the work of some of the present generation of leading poets writing in English, such as Paul Durcan and Paul Muldoon.

It is important to state the obvious: the poets mentioned here are predominantly Northern and male. It is not coincidental, surely, that recent years have seen substantial critical attention being paid to the idea of 'northern poetry'. The refined, expanded, and more self-consciously literary work of these poets is directly linked to the inheritance and influence that Kavanagh's poetry and prose continue to exert, almost as an orthodoxy. It should also be apparent, given the currency of the term 'northern poetry', that poets like Louis MacNeice, Michael Longley, Derek Mahon, and Tom Paulin are, by some way, distanced from this inheritance. They often address it, but they do not speak *out* of it.

Consequently it is surely an oversimplification to speak of 'northern poetry' as a homogeneous grouping prefixed by region and enfranchised by political or cultural proximities separate from the rest of the country. The imaginative 'initiative' has roamed more erratically and less conveniently than such an ascription would allow and seems to be asserting itself, on several different levels, in the terms of Kinsella's remarks on the Irish writer. This is not, I think, a matter of speculation or of current fad, but rather a feeling for the basis of attempts being made to explore other facets of experience and imaginative ideals such as one sees in the work of, say, Eavan Boland and Paul Durcan. Nor have I succumbed, I trust, to that process upon which John Berger wrote: 'I have come to see that the arranging of artists in a hierarchy of merit is an idle and essentially dilettante process. What matters are the needs which art answers.'[14]

The 'needs' that Berger refers to are coexistent with an audience's 'expectations' of what a poem is, what it should deal with and in what form. In Ireland, as Michael D. Higgins suggests, writers (and particularly poets) have been especially conscious of these expectations. This consciousness has been double-edged: of accepting (or acquiescing in) formal conventions and of formally fulfilling needs and expectations. There is not, so far as I know, anything 'wrong' with this. It has contributed to the popularity of poetry in Ireland, a consciousness that poetry is being written and that it is, in some manner of means, of importance. Precisely how it is important is left generously vague. Such a situation could imperceptibly, but significantly, degenerate into a self-delighting but obedient wit.

We have reached a point, possibly through the trauma of the late 1970s and 1980s, where the Irish past and the silted nets of convention are finally becoming untangled. More poets are unwilling to accept the pervasive experience of the past, without first questioning its relevance to them as creative individuals. The historical precedents that are available through

---

14 John Berger, *Art and Revolution* (London: Writer & Readers Co-op, 1969), prefacing note.

other literatures and cultures, as uncertain in direction as our own, are also being seriously considered.

In concluding her introduction to Walter Benjamin's *Illuminations*, Hannah Arendt wrote:

> Any period to which its own past has become as questionable as it has to us must eventually come up against the phenomenon of language, for in it the past is contained ineradicably, thwarting all attempts to get rid of it once and for all.[15]

In that almost throwaway phrase 'the phenomenon of language', we are 'up against' the crucial unexplored theme of Irish writing: not in the sense of labyrinthine Heideggerian disclosures, nor in the linguistic minutiae of dialect studies. The phenomenon of language in Ireland takes us back to the semantics of strife and the seeds of historical disaffection that continue to threaten the individual imagination by overshadowing the range and validity of its perceptions. In this 'confrontation', brief and secretive and arbitrary as it is, new ways of truth can be found, and therein lies the poet's responsibility: something that is outside the literal conventions and orthodoxies of our literary past. As Czeslaw Milosz wrote: 'The creative act is associated with a feeling of freedom that is, in its turn, born in the struggle against apparently invincible resistance.'[16]

[1983]

---

15   Hannah Arendt, *Illuminations*, 49.
16   Czeslaw Milosz, *The Captive Mind* (Harmondsworth: Penguin Books, 1980), 217.

CHAPTER 2

A Gritty Prod Baroque: Tom Paulin

I

From the opening poem, 'Under Creon', Tom Paulin's *Liberty Tree*[1] is an argument about history, its victims, and the unburied issues of the past that continue to haunt our present. It is an argument about justice and blame that Paulin has been conducting since his first book, A *State of Justice*,[2] followed by *The Strange Museum*.[3] Both books were well received, particularly in Britain. Here was a poet, English born but brought up in Belfast, educated there and in England, who offered a new perspective on Ireland. For a start, he was a Protestant and, as the poems showed, he was involved in the urban world, *not* the rural.

Paulin's poetry has, too, an intellectual sharpness – some might say, stringency – that is refreshing; his style has an Orwellian sense of suburban decay many critics find appealing. His poetry also fits a traditional English bill, but updated by a thoughtful integration within it of the modernist ethic of Mandelstam's poetry and of the figure of Mandelstam himself as symbolic of the Poet in the real Twentieth Century.

Comparison with Seamus Heaney's work is obvious on this level, but whereas Heaney delves down deep into the tangled roots of language, Paulin transplants them on to the construction site of history. His use of language is contractual, civic-minded, keeping his distance from the hothouse of what Heaney called 'our tribe's complicity'.[4] In a sense, Paulin

---

1 Tom Paulin, *Liberty Tree* (London: Faber and Faber, 1983).
2 Tom Paulin, *A State of Justice* (London: Faber and Faber, 1977).
3 Tom Paulin, *The Strange Museum* (London: Faber and Faber, 1980).
4 Seamus Heaney, 'Casualty', *Field Work* (London: Faber and Faber, 1979), 23.

cannot commit himself to the absurd, doomed, guilt-ridden 'Protestant' cause to stem what Heaney called, in 'At the Water's Edge', the 'scared, irrevocable steps'[5] of the just Catholic march of history.

To be able to speak with such confidence clearly bolsters a poet's self-image. Being denied this, the poet sees his landscape and language as somewhat irredeemable, marred by an oppressiveness of its own making; the poet speaks, therefore, of the seedy irrelevance of lower middle-class Protestantism in the last throes of its political hegemony and power.

Paulin's poetry holds itself off from delving into the material and psychic chaos of this background. His language is forced to make such contact neutral, observant, pointedly *un*engaged. The words themselves are adjectivally abstract, forming around the places and ideas of his poetry a bleak impressionism. Indeed, one picks at random words and phrases – 'stillness', 'forgiveness', 'politeness', 'blueness', 'greyness', 'graceless', 'worthless', 'dullness', 'colourless', 'whiteness', 'paleness', 'nameless', 'gentleness', 'bitterness', 'darkness', 'sadness', 'clearness', 'grey tenderness', 'banal sickness', 'banal stale atmosphere', 'taut dryness' – to illustrate Paulin's dependency upon stock poeticisms while the supply of his ideas is carried by the declamatory titles, narratives, and restrained confessions in another's voice.

If *The Strange Museum* was marked by Paulin's overemphasis, the kind of split level in which each poem dwelt, formally portraying scenes of similar proportion while the ideological theme-work went on down below, *Liberty Tree* bends under the weight of its own ambitious language. For it seeks to collapse the distinction between 'a dead light in the room' and where this leads to in *The Strange Museum*, 'the long lulled pause / Before history happens'. Pervasive moments of apprehension characterize the earlier volumes. In *Liberty Tree*, however, Paulin tries to weld together, in the very language he uses, the perceiving figure and scene of his poems with that which rules them – history. He is, in other words, not interested in stillnesses or pauses, but in a language that protests its own materiality, its perverse embroilment in history. For all the questioning of the earlier volumes, Paulin has found what I can only call a 'mock realism'; it is a change from historic Time to verbal Space and it takes him out of the picture.

---

5   Seamus Heaney, 'Triptych: III. At the Water's Edge', *Field Work*, 14.

Liberty Tree does not record speech, though; the poems are attempts to speak in 'the people's voice'. How does this show itself in the book? Again, at random, one comes up against words, phrases and, what seems to me, caricature, that keep the poetry on a very *literary* axis of being. These range from colloquialisms to a peculiar jargon I cannot quite place but which reminds me of the schoolboy comics and Christmas annuals that told tales of Imperial might in the idiom of Kipling.

I list those that strike me as being most illustrative of Paulin's lexicon. A 'scuffy sort of place', where *scuff* means to drag your feet thus damaging shoes; 'the biffy road', where *biff* is a thump in children's parlance, although I cannot make the connection with road; 'flups'; 'a farty hardboard hut' meaning *small* and *useless*. All of which come from 'Exogamy'.

In 'Descendancy', Paulin remarks that 'All those family histories / are like sucking a polo mint' and completes the analogy with, 'you're pulled right through / a tight wee sphincter / that loses you'.[6] The sense of the unselfconscious 'tight wee' drawn up beside the technical 'sphincter' is a deliberate act of Paulin's but I am unsure why: to domesticate 'sphincter' or to legitimize 'tight wee' and the community the phrase comes from? However one sees it, the object of 'Descendancy' gets reduced to a squabble over words that wrestle with each other as the meaning remains hidden in terms of specific conflict: 'Could be that a third one / – say an ex-B Special – / has pulled up at a road block / a shade far from Garrison?' This enigma remains so and the poem is validated extraneously by the factor of the present politico-cultural climate working in the poet's favour to explicate the matter.

One moves on to 'After the Summit' in which the first stanza opens with a peculiarly Belfast phrase, 'wee buns', meaning easily done, and proceeds into other colloquialisms like 'the boul Jimmy, your man Craig' and 'a dacent ould skin'.[7] The comprehending narrator of the second stanza recounts, like a voice-over, 'There is so little history / we must remember who we are.' But from the appropriated vitality of the language in the first stanza to the solemnity of the second, we get little choice in making

---

6   Tom Paulin, 'Descendancy', *Liberty Tree*, 20.
7   Tom Paulin, 'After the Summit', *Liberty Tree*, 29.

our own minds up as to what is actually going on in the poem. Its frame of reference is sealed shut with that dogmatic and far from self-justifying conclusion that preaches to us.

Who are 'we', for instance? 'We' are the Protestants of Northern Ireland, as poems like 'Desertmartin' and 'Descendancy' testify. Yet, time and again, I am forced back to the devices Paulin uses to depict their reality. Consider, for example, the second stanza of 'Politik':

> I'd be *dead chuffed* if I could catch
> the dialects of those sea-loughs,
> but I'm scared of all that's hard
> and completely subjective.[8]   [my italics]

The vernacular *dead chuffed* rises out of the poem in brash self-consciousness, but then its very essence in the poem is challenged by the poet's wish to do what he has actually achieved – to use, from 'the dialects' one term of reference: 'dead chuffed'. So it is confusing to confess that he is *scared* of that world while, simultaneously, making deliberate use of parts of its language. The poet really cannot have it both ways. Only out of the control of the 'completely subjective' can any true grasp of a people's language and, consequently their experience, emerge. This involves empathy, an artistic enterprise of conflicting proportion that may well lead, ironically, into a radically formal diction rather than the highly formalized *unliterary* one that Paulin has created in *Liberty Tree*.

I do not sense, either, the necessary complication of feeling in this book. Paulin seems to have his mind made up, but the emotional range of the poetry is unexplored. Take 'Politik' again:

> ... those quartzy voices in the playground
> of a school called Rosetta Primary
> whose basalt and sandstone have gone
> like Napoleon into Egypt ...[9]

---

8   Tom Paulin, 'Politik,' *Liberty Tree,* ib.
9   Paulin, 'Politik,' 30.

The reader is left literally bereft, not knowing what to think because Paulin does not present himself in the poem to take responsibility for what he is actually feeling and saying. Instead, he is there to make the necessary connections, the expert monitoring on his 'carbon-dater' the abstract lives of shadowy people. But, since *Liberty Tree* deals so explicitly with 'a plain Presbyterian grace', we must expect something more than metaphorical ambiguities. This bothers me for two reasons: firstly, because the images of *Liberty Tree* will probably be accepted without much thought given to what they effectively say about the Protestant peoples of Northern Ireland; secondly, because I admire Paulin as a poet and feel that *Liberty Tree* represents only a partial flowering of his art.

My dispute with this book is over what I perceive to be a continuing resistance in Paulin's work to release, imaginatively, feelings and beliefs of a much more personal nature, engendered in the complex individual experience and the formative influence of being – or seeing oneself as being – a northern Protestant.

Out of the pores of that body politic must come the privatized guilts, fears, and hopes of men and women who symbolize, in all their bewildering, and widely perceived, ungracious belligerence, the modern state of homelessness. They represent, as William Faulkner's characters represent, the need to conquer an onerous fate and to reconstruct a sense of community outside themselves – tasks of a truly historic kind. This is not, I trust, the language of a false apocalypse and I certainly do not intend to use it as a spectacular rule against which to measure the imaginative accomplishment of *Liberty Tree*. But these tasks, or imaginative responsibilities, do order the emotional and social framework I bring to bear upon *Liberty Tree* and they make all the more forceful my impressions of how this book undermines its own real achievements. I see this most clearly in 'Off the Back of a Lorry', a short piece of twenty-one lines. The language moves from a laid-back detective-story jargon of 'two rednecks troughing / in a gleaming diner' to Paisley 'putting pen to paper in Crumlin jail'. The images are cinematic and, whatever associations we make with them, they coalesce in the poet's own stating of them as 'pured fictions'. The poem then turns accusingly:

> ... and like the small ads
> in a country paper

> they build a gritty
> sort of prod baroque
> I must return to
> like my own boke.[10]

This poem depresses me because it is a dead end and reflects in a totally negative way upon Paulin's real ability as a poet. It is a biased piece of demotic. As a poem, it hardly gets a chance to rise to its feet. The stills by which it develops are black and white and so they end up illuminating little other than the poet's seeming contempt for what he is writing *about*. I question again the use of language: the vernacular *prod* for Protestant camouflages the flippant exuberance of baroque, unless, eccentrically, the poet means by *gritty*, the original French of 'mis-shapen pearl' and, if so, where does that leave us – the unlikely action of the poet going back to his own *boke* (vomit)?

The faltering of nerve, or the pressure of other influences, has unsettled Paulin's artistic poise in too many of the poems of *Liberty Tree*. This unbalances the book, eclipsing such fine poems as 'Black Bread' and 'The Book of Juniper' by forcing arguments rather than revealing Paulin's artistic reasoning. I am confident, however, that broaching the dangers of unfashionable complicities will create a richly human art out of Paulin's quarrel with the past. To call on Yeats, as a last resort, it might be no harm for Paulin to quarrel a little bit more fervently with himself.

II

Sometimes I have this ridiculous dream. I am at a party twenty years from now. There is a woman talking at me in one of those Cherry Valley accents (the Belfast equivalent of Dublin's apocryphal DARTspeak) and she's telling me earnestly how many generations of her Protestant people have lived on this island and that she has just discovered Irish literature and

---

10   Tom Paulin, 'Off the Back of a Lorry,' *Liberty Tree*, 33.

that the other day too she bought a *bodhrán* for her husband. Meanwhile, over in the corner, a friend is patiently negotiating a debate he has had thousands of times before about the survival of the Irish language. By this time most of Belfast has dual signposts and street names, and learning classes have sprung up in several community colleges in the better-off districts and also in a few of the twilight zones: so-called because Protestants and Catholics are still occasionally beaten-up in these grey areas banking on to the new 'ghettos' – rambling, grass-verged estates bristling with explosive pride and embittered rage.

I nod and accept her newfound enthusiasm, but see out of the window beyond her, over the castellated view of roof and chimney top, a part of the city where I grew up. It is all changed by now but it has kept a grand prospect over the lough. This is a world that does not exist but it probably will – one day. I do not think I much care for it, although it would take an essay in itself to give my reasons why.

A different state of ambiguity exists in Paulin's *Ireland and the English Crisis*, a collection of essays and reviews concerning literature and politics: 'My own critical position is eclectic and is founded on an idea of an identity which has *as yet* no formal or institutional existence' [my italics].[11]

Paulin's state is a peculiarly personal one that sounds political and has the aura about it ('as yet') of historical necessity. He finds himself 'drawn to John Hume's eloquence, his humane and constitutional politics' and rebuking 'provincialism' (that tawny old hare), feels no longer 'either in Ireland or England, any hostility toward a southern insouciance'.[12]

I am not sure what this 'insouciance' means – 'that ironical manner … so characteristic of Dublin culture' or, perhaps, 'the deep hostility which much of that community [in the south] feels towards both communities in the north'?[13] Either way, Paulin's no longer feeling hostile to 'it' is of some note since he relates both to the 'Ireland' and the 'English Crisis' of his title. Precisely *how* these link up is stated: 'In moments of aggravation it seems to me that if England no longer wants both the canon of English

---

11 Tom Paulin, *Ireland and the English Crisis* (Newcastle upon Tyne: Bloodaxe Books, 1984), 17.
12 Paulin, *Ireland and the English Crisis*, 16.
13 See 'The Making of a Loyalist,' 24–25.

literature *and* the desperate, wrecked state of Northern Ireland, then perhaps something could be created out of this double rejection?'[14]

The connection rests upon an even more tenuous relatedness than these 'moments of aggravation'. In his introduction, from which the two main quotations above are taken, Paulin writes, '*Once* a full Irish identity has been established *then* some form of sceptical detachment ... becomes necessary and obligatory [my italics].'[15]

I would have thought it 'necessary and obligatory' for a writer to stick to the truth that he knows and that this obligation is paramount, 'sceptical detachment' or no. It certainly is not welded programmatically to 'a full Irish identity', as if the latter were like 'a full Irish breakfast'.

Like people, the imagination is not logical; it is often drawn to what repels it. 'Then' does not *necessarily* exist – it depends upon what people think, feel, experience, and interpret. And a writer cannot surely postdate his own experience or lock parts of it away until some possible state of grace or some political 'solution' designates the establishment of 'a full Irish identity'. I was surprised, too, that Paulin did not take this opportunity to examine his own assertion: 'A recognition that the Irish writer who publishes in Britain has a neo-colonial identity. And the central question which faces the neo-colonial writers is – whom am I writing for?'[16]

Is it that transparently obvious – for what about the audience to whom such a question is itself pitched? And there are other questions that hardly ruffle the sleeve of *Ireland and the English Crisis*. Paulin writes, again in the introduction, that 'most Unionists have a highly selective memory and cling desperately to a raft constructed from two dates – 1690 and 1912. The result is an unusually fragmented culture and a snarl of superficial or negative attitudes. A provincialism of the most disabling kind.'[17]

But Paulin's reluctance to distinguish between 'Unionism' and the complex reasons why ordinary people in the north of Ireland feel themselves to be 'British' rather than 'Irish' is a crucial oversight. Calling it 'that mythic consumer durable' (feeling *British*, not *Irish*) does not get us far

---

14 Paulin, *Ireland and the English Crisis*, 15.
15 Paulin, *Ireland and the English Crisis*, 18.
16 Paulin, *Ireland and the English Crisis*, 18.
17 Paulin, *Ireland and the English Crisis*, 17.

in understanding why so many people in the North want to stay 'British' while, before their very eyes, their homes, factories, and that elusive 'way of life', corrode into a brittle and unsustainable formalism.

There is, though, nothing 'unusually fragmented' about the Ulster Protestant cultures; its 'selectivity' is common enough in these islands and the 'snarl' a conventional target easily transferable to other locations. I can still see, for instance, the bloodlessly ecstatic face of a well-known Irish journalist at some literary reception, stuck into my own with the self-satisfied words, 'Doesn't your own lot usually kill their traitors!'

Paulin hits the point with 'disabling', but its context is dismissive and neglects the sympathetic justice of criticism such as one finds in Sarah Nelson's *Ulster's Uncertain Defenders: Loyalists and the Northern Ireland Conflict*.[18] Indeed, the entire thrust of *Ireland and the English Crisis* abandons the present condition and history of such people (the million or so) in favour of raising literary questions about being an Irish writer 'with his neo-colonial identity'. I would have thought the other matter is much more pressing, if less popular, as the war in the North drags relentlessly on, claiming the lives of young men and women and making the conventional sense of 'Ireland' as a historical community a very sick joke.

Paulin is right in much of what he says in this book. And it is nice to '*assume* the existence of a non-sectarian, republican state which comprises the whole island of Ireland [my italics].' In Ireland, many assume it every day and fight for it in many different and, often, costly ways: women's health issues, sheltering the poor and homeless, protecting the rights of minorities, restoring to a fuller life those suffering from drug and alcohol abuse, resisting the decay of rural towns and villages, coping with emigration and battling for the civil and social rights of the unemployed. But it would be naïve to assume that the major block to the establishment 'of a non-sectarian republican state' comes solely from Unionists or the grim reapers in the British state. The political and religious power structures in the present Republic and *its* exclusivist social legislation are as determinedly

---

18   Sarah Nelson, *Ulster's Uncertain Defenders: Loyalists and the Northern Ireland Conflict* (Belfast: Appletree Press, 1984).

against such a non-sectarian 'republican' state in practice as were the miserable and bigoted policies of the party that once governed in the North.

Along with Paulin, I wish to see the neighbouring country across the water 'fully multi-racial, nuclear-free and more socially just'. But, again, in the world where we actually live it is not simply a matter of choice, even with such a harmless option as this one. And we are only kidding ourselves (and fooling no one else) if we think it can be any different for a writer, including those whom Paulin discusses in *Ireland and the English Crisis* – Joyce, Yeats, MacNeice, Auden, and Kavanagh. Paulin brings this shifting contradiction fully into focus. There may be too many short pieces but with excellent essays like 'The Making of a Loyalist', 'National Myths', 'The Writer Underground', 'English Now', and 'Paisley's Progress', *Ireland and the English Crisis* is a pioneering step taken by an Irish poet into the minefield of literary and social criticism.

III

In *The Faber Book of Political Verse*, however, Paulin labours under the strain of too much literary self-consciousness. Possibly as a result of the state of literary affairs in England (which he charted in *Ireland and the English Crisis*), Paulin's anthology is a personal selection of poems that can be only roughly categorized as 'political'.[19]

The introduction is full of imperatives ('must' is commonplace) and condemnation, implied or overt – Hopkins's head rolls, for instance, 'as a right-wing patriot'. *Links* are forged by the new time, *traditions* established, *influences* traced, and unspecified factors abound, such as the 'certain intent cadence' of Yeats or his 'more brutal qualities', as well as 'certain imaginative positives in Heaney' or 'certain schools of literary criticism'. One yearns for specifics.

Editorial static is earthed, however, by standard literary complaints: 'In the Western democracies it is still possible for many readers, students and

---

19   *The Faber Book of Political Verse*, ed. Tom Paulin (London: Faber and Faber, 1986).

teachers of literature to share the view that poems exist in a timeless vacuum or a soundproof museum, and that poets are gifted with an ability to hold themselves above history, rather like skylarks or weather satellites.'[20]

Is this really true of the vast bulk of schools and colleges throughout Europe, Britain, or Ireland? In the majority of such places, the poet is read as a writer of processable footnotes to historical events, personal scenes from life, or as a painter of definable landscapes: all very much giving up students to boredom and the fidgets as poems are learnt as *facts*, but not of poets being 'timeless' or 'above history'. This is a problem 'the Poet' encounters far more than the reader.

In contrast with this, there is 'the ironic gravity and absence of hope in poets such as Herbert, Rozewicz, Holub [that] reminds us that in eastern Europe the poet has a responsibility both to art and to society, and that this responsibility is single and indivisible'.

I do not quibble with this but, rather, with the overdetermination of categories and tradition-making that Paulin goes in for in his introduction. A poet like Elizabeth Bishop is squeezed into place as 'patrician' and as 'a social critic' whose 'sophisticated quietism' makes her 'a silent political poet', in spite of herself! It is a lack of discretion to assume the mantle of speaking on behalf of 'we in the west' as a people 'who have difficulty in comprehending' the plight of fellow human beings in the east and that 'we … too readily twist to our own smug purposes' the message these poets send. Who are 'we'?

Moving from the introduction, the selection of poems is quixotic. One wonders about the predominant influence of the Irish contingent – in comparison with the relatively small presence of those established 'political' European poets saluted in the introduction. A poem apiece from Brecht, Enzensberger, and Holub, but five poems from Seamus Heaney, three from Derek Mahon, two from Paul Muldoon, and contributions from a motley crew of Aogán Ó Rathaille, Fear Dorcha Ó Meallain, Swift, Joyce, Yeats, Longley, and Deane. Pablo Neruda pips it with one poem, as does Pasternak; while Anna Akhamatova's single poem is one of six translations contributed by the editor. Tony Harrison – the most directly political poet

---

20 Paulin, Introduction to *The Faber Book of Political Verse*, 17.

writing in England today – has one poem, which keeps him in the company of Berryman, Bishop, Eliot, Frost, Hill, Hughes, Lawrence, and Owen.

On the other hand, poets like Jeffrey Wainwright and Christopher Middleton do not feature at all. Nor do any of the 'political' poets like Pádraic Fiacc, John Montague, Brendan Kennelly, Paul Durcan, or James Simmons, while neither 'Nightwalker' nor 'Butcher's Dozen' by Thomas Kinsella gets a look in.

The selections are perplexing. Perhaps Dryden's 'Absalom and Achitophel' *is* 'a great masterpiece' but trying to convince teachers and students that it does not 'exist in a soundproof museum' is another day's work. In any case, John Cooper Clarke's fashionable hype of 'the fucking days are fucking long' is *not* a masterpiece.

Whether or not 'a popular verse tradition' appears to be extinct in England may prove a rum point in 'certain circles' but, given the absence of contemporary Irish ballads and songs, Paulin has missed the chance to include popular works like 'The Men Behind the Wire', 'Take Me Home to Mayo', or 'The Ballad of Bobby Sands'. One is left with Paulin's declared 'hope' that this book will 'contribute towards the creation of a broad "canon" of political verse in English'. If the 'polemical introduction', which, the preface says, Craig Raine ('who commissioned the anthology') 'provoked', had been shortened from its thirty-seven pages, more space might have been found for *poems* rather than for the call to arms of 'canon-fodder'.

IV

If *The Faber Book of Political Verse* is marred by a missionary self-consciousness, Paulin's fourth volume of poems, *Fivemiletown*, carries a similar burden. Before turning to the poems, however, it might be useful to take a look at the assumptions that surround the book. This is the back-cover blurb:

> [Paulin] continues his exploration of the Northern Irish predicament, but at an even higher pitch of risk than he attempted before. The theme of Protestant identity is

considered in both local and global terms, and Paulin's devices which here range from the most measured and laconic statements, to utterances that threaten to defy all formal constraints, demonstrate the radical nature of his response to a major cultural crisis. *Fivemiletown* is an astonishing and explosive performance.[21]

The 'higher pitch of risk' should put the reader on guard, because writing poetry in these islands rarely involves personal *risk*, only the possibility of artistic failure. As in the past, Paulin has not been well served by his blurb writers. Here, one jibs at such clarion calls as 'utterances that threaten to defy all formal constraints' – which sounds like a blood vessel about to burst – while the 'radical nature' of Paulin's 'response to a major cultural crisis' asks more questions than one book of poetry can ever hope to answer and, maybe, should ever try. What does *radical* mean in this context – using short lines and what used to be called 'bad language'? A radical *poet* is someone, like Brian Coffey, who recasts the language. And which particular 'major cultural crisis' are we being referred to here – the breakup of Britain? The acceptable face of violence in the North? *Fivemiletown* does not disclose these things.

Having read and re-read the book, I am not sure either what it has to do with the declared 'theme of Protestant identity … considered in both local and global terms'. Since when were poets supposed to state their themes, anyway, outside the seminar room? And the 'Northern Irish predicament': *predicament*?

Following *Liberty Tree*, Paulin has continued writing 'dialect poems'. These are not just taken from *his* perceptions of how English is spoken in the North but, also, from how it is spoken in Britain by intellectuals who read poetry and write about it. There are, for example, a lot of words italicized in *Fivemiletown*. This denotes meaning over and above the poem's own proven significance. Words like *sdark*, *sput*, *whap*, and others. Foreign phrases are liberally scattered through the book as well: 'mon cabinetnoir', 'Kurbishutte', 'Schwarzerd', and 'differance'. There also continues to be a subtext of literary chat about speech, the demotic, reading, and the declaration, in one of the poems from and about writers:

21   Tom Paulin, *Fivemiletown* (London: Faber and Faber, 1987).

> – I'm letting you off the hook, Albion,
> not for your own sake, never,
> but because out of your steam presses
> shot Dickens, Darwin, Spencer and Mill![22]

What differentiates *Fivemiletown* from previous collections is the vigorous use of four-letter words and sexuality. There are lots of 'fucks', 'fucking', 'a drunken fuck', and quick blow jobs.

We also read of 'the operation / on the Dauphin's foreskin', 'left testicles' crop up in the same poem, while in a half-dozen poems or so Paulin returns mechanically to sex and sexual encounters. Whether doing 'it best / in the bath' or 'meeting in this room / with no clothes on – to believe in nothing / to be nothing', there is a strained, oddly formal *angst* in evidence. While the hard man in *Fivemiletown* steps out from the screwing fairly chastened, there is good old northern ire in his belly: 'how the fuck', 'shit scared', and 'why give a shit'.

There is something far too contrived about Paulin's outrage and use of language in this book. This self-consciousness contrasts sharply with, say, the prose writing of Dermot Healy; the need to appear crude, to show ordinary people in the throes of real life, strikes me as an understandable but dated reaction against the Gentility Principle. Who uses terms such as 'lunk July', 'bum hour', 'scroggy town', 'gummy warmth', 'yompy farts', 'dwammy sick', or the cold expression of an 'oral childhood'?

One tires of the quizzically knowing semantics and, eventually, impatience grows into disbelief that this is where we have ended up:

> ... that story with its thoughtful prisoner,
> miles of salt-marsh and a word like *wesh*.[23]

Floating in the background of *Fivemiletown* is a pissed-off figure. The book seems to hover with 'him' between disenchantment and disgust, without ever artistically revealing *why*. We are to take all this on faith.

While the good poems struggle for a bit of air ('The Red Handshake', 'André Chenier', 'Peacetime', 'We're the Rosenberg', 'Voronezh', and 'An

---

22 Paulin, 'From *Landsflykt*,' *Fivemiletown*, 45.
23 Paulin, 'Mythologies,' *Fivemiletown*, 26.

Ulster Unionist Walks the Streets'), the rest thrash around, bearing grand titles like 'Defenester' and 'The Defenestration of Hillsborough' until 'The Caravans of Luneberg Heath' and Heidegger's miserable duplicities summon the end and the following haunting lines:

> – but what nature is
> and what's natural
> I can never tell just now[24]

I think it is a shame that Tom Paulin, a poet whom I greatly admire and will continue to do so in spite of the worst that *Fivemiletown* can offer, is barking up the wrong tree. Inspiration must lie elsewhere.

V

In that marvellously committed and lopsided book, *ABC of Reading*, Ezra Pound blasts: 'The critic who doesn't make a personal statement is merely an unreliable critic. He is not a measurer but a repeater of other men's results.'[25] Much of what goes for criticism at present is either unreliable self-serving puff or heavy-duty world-view-enforcement. Which is to say, we know the opinion beforehand. It's rare for a literary critic to speak his or her mind about how good a book is and why.

Tom Paulin's television appearances on the BBC's 'Late Review' are certainly a measure of *his* critical forthrightness and willingness to call a dud a dud. The vernacular performance of bemused seriousness translates, however, oddly to the page. Some of the essays in *Writing to the Moment: Selected Critical Essays 1980–1996* are reprinted from Paulin's Bloodaxe collection *Ireland and the English Crisis*.[26] They stand up well, particularly the politico-cultural ones: 'The Making of a Loyalist' (1980)

---

24 Paulin, 'Now for the Orange Card,' *Fivemiletown*, 11.
25 Ezra Pound, *ABC of Reading* (London: Faber and Faber, 1951), 30.
26 Tom Paulin, *Writing to the Moment: Selected Critical Essays 1980–1996* (London: Faber and Faber, 1996).

on Conor Cruise O'Brien is remarkably prescient, given Dr O'Brien's alignment with the absurdly entitled UK Unionists; 'Paisley's Progress' (1982) is the best thing written on the subject; and short pieces on Louis MacNeice and Derek Mahon are sharp, concise, and helpful. The bigger statements seem dated and constrained by polemical self-consciousness and a curious anxiety to prove something: 'A New Look at the Language Question', 'Political Verse', and 'Vernacular Verse', brashly identify the intellectual coordinates of Paulin's extensive reading of poetry. The individual poet's art (never mind personality) fades into a structurally articulated plan of action: Elizabeth Bishop's 'sophisticated quietism – or her radical distaste – challenges the democratic Yankee triumphalism of much American verse'; 'Blues singers' are considered as 'the most authentic American political poets' whose 'work challenges the more comfortable written tradition'. Yes, but … The frank, clear prose and the eye for political deceit and the culturally dubious make *Writing to the Moment* a powerful gathering of Paulin's formidable and erudite conceptualizing of literature, its place in this moment, and what he calls, in the title essay, 'a refusal of the literary': the enabling (and self-dramatizing) idea of much of what Paulin writes as both poet and critic. Ireland features quite a bit ('Where the Aran Islands used to be the focus of cultural authenticity, Belfast would now [1987] seem to be the deep navel of ethnic chutzpah.'[27] [*Oops*]) and England, mostly of the nineteenth and early twentieth centuries.

Surprisingly, judgements of contemporary poets and prose writers are few and far between. Of Tony Harrison, for instance, a poet and dramatist one would think was close to Paulin's own artistic and intellectual concerns, not much more than a passing reference. The harping on about dialect, local words, argot of one kind or another, and the rattling around for challenges to 'the more comfortable written tradition' belies an old-fashioned romance with 'orality', the spoken tradition, the natural voice, which strays very close to Colour Supplementalese: 'Reading these lines "You shall have a fishy / in a little dishy / you shall have a fishy / when the boat comes in" we need to hear "boat" not as *bot*, but as the Northumbrian bisyllabic *bo-uht*.' Paulin's distaste for what he calls southern Irish writers'

---

27   Paulin, 'The Crack,' *Writing to the Moment*, 96–97.

'saccharine gabbiness' is fair enough, but the notion that the vernacular is a sure sign of artistic authenticity and a radically acceptable civic consciousness (in Britain or Ireland) should have been left out to dry years back:

> A writer who employs a word like 'geg' or 'gulder' or Kavanagh's lovely 'gobshite' [*lovely?*] will create a form of closed, secret communication with readers who come from the same region. These words act as a kind of secret sign and serve to exclude the outside world. They constitute a dialect of endearment within the wider dialect.[28]

These informed essays know exactly what they are about; Paulin's rational discourse is copybook stuff. While at no stage does he actually challenge received reputations or provoke reassessments of forgotten or neglected writers, the spirit of *Writing to the Moment* is very much of these times, and Tom Paulin one of the wizards of 'Uz'.

[1984–1996]

---

28   Paulin, 'A New Look at the Language Question,' *Writing to the Moment*, 65.

CHAPTER 3

Northern Windows/Southern Stars

I

One can get a fair idea of how 'Modern Irish Literature' came into being, reading these diverse and differently enjoyable books as a historical sequence – Richard Ellmann's *Four Dubliners*, Frank Ormsby's *Northern Windows,* and John Ryan's *Remembering How We Stood*.[1] From William Carleton (1794–1869), we move through his rural Ulster aspirations to become a Man of Letters in Dublin while Ellmann's opening chapter takes us from Wilde in 1870s Oxford to Joyce in Switzerland (1917–1919). Following on we have, in Ormsby's anthology, the northern voices of John Boyd's Belfast in the 1920s, Ellmann's Yeats in 1934 with his virility problems, and the angles of Robert Greacen, Sam McAughtry, and John Harbinson on Belfast in the 1930s, before Louis MacNeice's 1941 recollections of his upbringing in County Antrim bring us to the watershed of the Second World War, where Beckett concludes *Four Dubliners*. During the war and onwards we have, in Ryan's recollections (first published in 1975), Brendan Behan, Patrick Kavanagh, and Brian O'Nolan sequestered in McDaid's bar, while Michael Longley's memory, in *Northern Windows*, spans the late 1930s in Belfast to the present, with the Devlins – Polly and Bernadette- and Robert Johnstone bringing the picture up to the late 1950s and early 1960s.

---

1   Richard Ellmann, *Four Dubliners: Wilde, Yeats, Joyce and Beckett* (London: Hamish Hamilton, 1987), Frank Ormsby, *Northern Windows* (Belfast: Blackstaff Press, 1987), John Ryan, *Remembering How We Stood* (Mullingar: Lilliput Press, 1987 [orig. ed. 1975]).

Ryan's memoirs, Ormsby's autobiographical selections, and Ellmann's recast lectures splice into each other in provocatively contrary ways. The slow embrace of Ryan's sketches contrasts with Ormsby's carefully monitored portrait gallery against which the incisive studies of Ellmann's book appear on a different critical wavelength. Both Ormsby and Ryan, as editor and memorialist respectively, are affectionate and unassuming in regard to their subjects, although Ryan does force the pace a bit concerning 'reputations' and his being at the centre of things.

Ellmann's distance is impeccable. What emerges from *Four Dubliners* is a cool, objective rendering that shows the individual writers as people of their time. Paradoxically, while being powerfully rooted in one particular place ('Ulster') at various times along a chronological continuum, *Northern Windows* misses the same style of definition, with the uniqueness of the individuals blurring under actual accounts of childhood and growing up in the province. In some way, we do not actually see more of either the place or the people through *Northern Windows* but, rather, find confirmation of historical realities as we already know them to be. It is a book of reassurance.

Northern Windows reveals a kind of unwritten, mutual reserve in which feelings are treated like ideas and ideas turn into family attitudes best not brought out into the open. In a mystifying way, the meaning of sectarianism is not really probed, even while it remains a central fact of northern life. Lives are, of course, lived in spite of such a human blight but rarely in these contributions is there a sense of what sectarianism does to everyone concerned. We do not gain any deeper feeling for the complex emotional and sexual taboos that were, and still are, a basic feature of the religious and social life in the North. This is not a criticism of *Northern Windows* as a book but, rather, of the similar views of the world that emerge from it.

The novelists and poets whose stories largely go to make up *Northern Windows* – Carleton, Shane F. Bullock, Forrest Reid, George Buchanan, Patrick Kavanagh, Louis MacNeice, Sam Hanna Bell, John Boyd, Robert Greacen, Michael Longley, and Robert Johnstone – all give entertaining accounts of their past. They read well but we are not – really – hearing the half of it.

In *Remembering How We Stood*, Ryan's reserve proves liberating, yet candor can lead him into the grand statement, meticulously avoided by all the northerners: 'Writers and artists are endemically quarrelsome; their occupation makes them more distraught and susceptible to hysteria than other professionals; because of art's insecurity and the wounds that the morbidly intelligent inflict upon themselves.'[2]

This sounds like hypochondria, the sleeping sickness of the imagination; but is the 'occupation' of being a writer really more prone to hysteria than, say, that of a politician, a dentist, a quantity surveyor, a housewife, or a football player? The question collapses under the weight of assumption and cliché the contemporary writer must come to terms with concerning both how he or she should act and what he or she is expected to write about. As Ryan says of Behan: 'He seemed to be wired-up to the media.'[3] Public perceptions of poets and poetry are, for instance, generally related to the myth that there is in Ireland 'a standing army' of poets, one of Patrick Kavanagh's 'great' sayings. Even though such a myth can be easily dismissed – by comparison with how many spinsters, retired Yorkshire majors, and Cornish rectors are religiously firing off their poems to the literary magazines – it has a life of its own, owing mainly to the bland recycling of such 'sayings' of this writer or that as a substitute for genuine criticism.

Hysteria is not, of course, closer to the artist than to any other human being. Artists struggle, often with more failure than success, to embody and carry over into their work pressures of, and upon, the self and society. In Ireland, the problem is our basic uncertainty about the value of the literary work (which standards should we use, for instance? are there any?), whereas the public role and social occasion of its expression are more readily assimilated as 'stories' and recognized with the standard epithets like 'great' or 'a genius'. This avoids the awkward business of assessing, questioning, considering, and vindicating artistic worth, leaving these to anecdote. As with politics in Ireland, personality often means much more, and thence to the ghastly patronage of 'the character'. Louis MacNeice spotted this when he remarked upon the paradox in Joyce, that while 'a master of written

2 Ryan, 157.
3 Ryan, 72.

dialogue' like Eliot, he remained 'essentially literary and neither of them could be described as a sparkling conversationalist.... It is ironic that the greatest celebrant of Dublin should have been so lacking in the Dubliner's most famous virtue or vice.'[4]

The bulk of our generalizations about art, writing, and the imagination reflect this distinct critical unease. So the poet must 'suffer' and be seen to suffer: Kavanagh in his miserable Dublin bachelor flat is an identifiable image, whereas Joyce, attended by friends and well-wishers in a French apartment, is not. The price of recognition is located somewhere between priest (vocation) and vagabond (dislocation); reverence with piety, a fateful mix at the best of times. The cost this exacts as regards reality is colossal, yet Irish writers have been prone to accept these terms, petulantly but inevitably; or else fly the coop, as many from Wilde's time on have indeed done. Ellmann's chapter on Samuel Beckett, for example, records:

> At the age of twenty-two Beckett went from Dublin to Paris; twenty-six years before, at the age of twenty, Joyce made the same journey. Equally pivotal were the displacements of Yeats at twenty-two from Dublin to London, and of Wilde, at twenty, from Dublin to Oxford. The geographical change symbolised for all four of them an attempt to proceed from the known to the unknown, to remake themselves in unfamiliar air.[5]

There is, too, a telling moment in Louis MacNeice's autobiography, *The Strings Are False*, when in 1939, having travelled around the west of Ireland and heard in Galway the news of the outbreak of war, he spends a final few days in Dublin:

> ... I was alone with the catastrophe, spent Saturday drinking in a bar with Dublin literati; they hardly debated the war but debated the correct versions of Dublin street songs.... The intelligentsia continued their parties, their mutual malice was as effervescent as ever. There was still a pot of flowers in front of Matt Talbot's shrine, the potboy priests and the birds of prey were still the dominant caste; the petty bureaucracy continued powerful and petty.[6]

4   Louis MacNeice, *Selected Literary Criticism of Louis MacNeice*, ed. Alan Heuser (Oxford: Clarendon Press, 1987), 214.
5   Ellmann, *Four Dubliners: Wilde, Yeats, Joyce and Beckett*, 79–80.
6   Louis MacNeice, *The Strings Are False* (London: Faber and Faber, 1982), 212.

It was during this period – the late 1930s to the mid-1950s – that current popular images of poets and poetry took root in Ireland. Possibly because poets were prominent in the struggle that achieved the nominal political and economic independence of the Irish Free State from the British Empire, their profile has remained consistently more visible than, say, that of playwrights, novelists, or visual artists. However, if one takes the four Dubliners of Richard Ellmann's book (Wilde, Yeats, Joyce, and Beckett), we do not associate them with either the 'hysteria' Ryan sees as the hallmark of writers or, in their maturity, as Dublin pub literati.

The public perception of these four people is as *artists*. While these perceptions may be influenced by Wilde's homosexuality, Yeats's love affair with Maud Gonne and his presumed arrogance, Joyce's exiled 'love-hate' relationship with the country, or Beckett's remoteness and 'obscure' plays, their acknowledgment remains as artists.

When we turn to Behan, O'Nolan, and Kavanagh, the three Dublin-based writers who figure in *Remembering How We Stood*, we read of a demonstrative yet repressed existence in which drink plays the dominant part. Frustration and grievance dog their every achievement.

The men of John Ryan's book (women rarely feature) are caught between heroes and ideals on the one hand and, on the other, the country as it was in the 1940s and 1950s, closed off from the world, maintaining a phony diplomatic status quo that, afterwards, slumped into the deplorable exodus of people in search of a decent standard of living elsewhere after the war (or 'the Emergency' as it was known in 'the Free State').

The writers who remained in Ireland during this time had their work cut out for them but, as Ryan's memoirs recall, they were part of a wider supportive community, albeit a literary one. For Denis Devlin, Brian Coffey, Samuel Beckett, even Seán O'Faoláin, Francis Stuart, or Louis MacNeice, their separation wrote them out of the Irish literary 'scene', and, largely, continues to do so.

In *Remembering How We Stood*, John Ryan, having established the mood of the time, accords to his friends a heroism of sorts: 'We shared the experience of working together in besieged times when the worst enemy was the one within the gates. They were the keepers of the nation's conscience.'⁷

I dare say Joyce would have had none of this, even though it was he who proposed that we forge the uncreated conscience of the race. Stephen Dedalus, though, was a very idealistic young man. According to Ellmann, Joyce wanted ordinary people 'to know themselves as they really were, not as they were taught by church and state to be. He gave dignity to the common life that we all share.'⁸

It is this dignity that a writer can harm most because it is his own but, stripped of the sense of having a place in common with his peers, a shared life, the writer eventually reacts against that society in whatever way is the most accessible and meaningful to it. All too often in Ireland, 'drink' has been that symbolic gesture of rejection – rejecting the self, the home, the marriage, the restrictions of life, real or imagined. It is hardly stretching the point to see Behan, Kavanagh, and Brian O'Nolan as *victims* of this particular cultural malaise.

Now things have changed. As Thomas Kilroy remarked in his essay 'The Irish Writer: Self and Society, 1950–80':

> The public position of a Seamus Heaney, a John McGahern, a Brian Friel is manifestly different to that of a Brian Coffey, a Patrick Kavanagh, a Brinsley MacNamara. The change has to do with the earnestness, the sometimes gauche and embarrassing earnestness, with which the Irish public in these decades has strained towards its particular conception of modernity.⁹

Homing in on Kavanagh as representative, Kilroy describes him stalking 'through the fifties like some *cainteoir* [vagrant satirist] out of the Gaelic past with that sartorial stamp, the swinging coat, the dipped brooding hat, the notorious cough and splutter, arms akimbo, knotted like an embrace that has lost or crushed its loved object'.¹⁰ 'It will be the business of the biographer', Kilroy concludes, 'to analyse the kind of distortions of

---

7   Ryan, 19.
8   Ellmann, *Four Dubliners: Wilde, Yeats, Joyce and Beckett*, 76.
9   Thomas Kilroy, 'The Irish Writer: Self and Society, 1950–80,' in *Literature and the Changing Ireland*, ed. Peter Connolly (Bucks: Colin Smythe, 1982), 177–178.
10 Kilroy, *Literature and the Changing Ireland*, 186.

selfhood which Kavanagh affected in his role as a poet and to question the kind of society which impelled him, often with great cruelty and delight in the histrionics, towards a perverse form of self-satisfaction on the part of society itself.'[11] It is a society still with us today, even though the strain towards modernity is less anxious.

II

Circumstances have, however, all too often led us into a rigid force of habit, detached from what is actually going on in Irish society. In this regard, Sarah Nelson makes a simple but crucial point: 'Conflicts and solutions are played out by real people; to examine their feelings and experiences is to restate the importance of people, not as pawns in a historical process but as actors who respond to and influence events.'[12]

Over the years Ireland, north and south, has come in for an exorbitant amount of attention. Writers have been urged to become guru-like figures addressing 'historical problems'; talking about themselves and their work is now an expected element in Irish writing. Somehow, though, the sharp edge of criticism, the exploration of the structure and contemporary meaning of a writer's work, has blurred into a 'themed' mist. Reality – what is happening and why – is shunted off into an adjunct of writing, like an afterthought.

Yet the central facts of life in Ireland remain: the eruption and continuation for a quarter of a century of political upheaval in Northern Ireland, matched by deep-seated social, moral, and sexual tensions and resentments in the Republic. 'The Troubles' are unquestionably the watershed in recent Irish history. Life changed irrevocably, both directly and indirectly, for hundreds of thousands, including my own generation, who inherited ordinary hopes for the future only to see these break up in the grim squalor of daily bombings and nightly assassinations. A wedge has been driven into

---

11   Kilroy, *Literature and the Changing Ireland*, 186.
12   Sarah Nelson, *Ulster's Uncertain Defenders* (Belfast: Appletree Press, 1984), 11.

the emotional life of that generation, between the past of the 1960s, when they were teenagers, and the present.

This rupture in time made of many exiles from their own youth, forcing them to look back, sometimes with nostalgia but, more often, with unflinching realism, to a time never allowed its chance. This sense of incompleteness will, I imagine, haunt many of us for the rest of our days. It has put paid to the assumption that life is a natural, linear process. As Czeslaw Milosz wrote in *The Captive Mind*:

> Man tends to regard the order he lives in as natural. The houses he passes on his way to work seem more like rocks rising out of the earth than products of human hands. He considers the work he does in his office or factory as essential to the harmonious functioning of the world.... His first stroll along a street littered with glass from bomb-shattered windows, shakes his faith in the 'naturalness' of his world.[13]

With that realization, the certainties also go. For the writers, it involves trying to remake connections between words and things within verifiable experience and not what these have been made to represent in the past.

It is refreshing, therefore, to read John Hewitt, who did not loll around in our hang-ups but got on with the job and kept his eye on what was literally going on around him:

> The careful rejection of the rhetorical and flamboyant, the stubborn concreteness of the imagery, the conscientious cleaving to objects of sense which, not at all paradoxically, provides the best basis and launching ground for the lonely ascents of practical mysticism which lie close to the heart of Ulster's best intellectual activity and make us bold enough to claim Concord as a townland of our own.[14]

This single-mindedness meant that Hewitt rarely let caricature and received opinion obstruct what he needed to say. Hewitt was, after all, a committed man who held to certain ideas, like regionalism and socialism, throughout his life. These ideas, particularly his socialism, cost

---

13   Czeslaw Milosz, *The Captive Mind* (Harmondsworth, Middlesex: Penguin Books, 1980), 25.
14   John Hewitt, *Ancestral Voices: The Selected Prose of John Hewitt*, ed. Tom Clyde (Belfast: Blackstaff Press, 1987), 111.

him dearly. Not surprisingly, they are the mainstays of *Ancestral Voices*, sometimes explicitly so, though sometimes unvoiced. The even-tempered manner of Hewitt's prose describes an attitude to the world that is always instructive:

> ... by the mid nineteen twenties, with the new ministries in gear and the non- entities trooping to the Westminster backbenches, it seemed evident that the Unionists were a right wing offshoot of the British Tory Party, who at home fought every election on the border, and that the Nationalists, the representatives of the Catholic minority, were merely obsolete clansmen with old slogans, moving in an irrelevant dream, utterly without the smallest fig-leaf of a social policy.[15]

As well as calling the political shots, *Ancestral Voices* doubles back to a real question that, curiously, casts doubt upon the very entity that Hewitt is credited with creating – the Ulster Writer:

> The Ulster ideology then offered the writer no inspiration. The Ulster public offered him no livelihood. Nor has the latter problem yet been solved. There must be very few writers who can be entirely dependent on writing, as apart from journalism, in the whole Irish island. Hence the writer is confronted with another highly personal question – how to make his art not merely an escape mechanism or recreation from his routine avocation; how to make his daily work provide a flow of experience usable in his art; or, at least, how to ensure that the nature and the demands of his calling do not smother his aesthetic sensibilities. These each must solve for himself but they can have their profitable side. Until he has absorbed a deal of human experience, no person is fit to write anything of value. If writers in an isolated group or in individual segregation are for too long disassociated from the social matrix, their work will inevitably grow thin and tenuous, more and more concerned with form than content, heading for marvellous feats of empty virtuosity.[16]

Behind the unassuming bearing of Hewitt the writer, one also senses restlessness and a probing self-consciousness. Hewitt well understood poetry as a powerful compensation for the inadequacies of the social reality that he had inherited and sought to transform; the personal life imaginatively

---

15 Hewitt, *Ancestral Voices: The Selected Prose of John Hewitt*, ed. Tom Clyde, 149.
16 Hewitt, *Ancestral Voices: The Selected Prose of John Hewitt*, ed. Tom Clyde, 114.

subdued, knowing its place in the scheme of things. Therein lies the struggle that Hewitt's writing represents against a collective inertia buried deep in the past, in his ancestral voices. It gives his writing an unforced edge of grace and constraint but, always, the humility of the true artist.

As Tom Clyde, the editor of *Ancestral Voices*, remarks, Hewitt's prose was 'driven by a need to define himself in terms of the past, both of his family and of his province, to dig out long-buried artists and rebels, to trace lines of descent, to forge his own personal mythology'.[17] This most honourable of men looked all around and thought what he could do to help. In a sense, his work can be summed up by Robert Lowell's description of Frost as a poet who 'somehow put life into a dead tradition'.[18] What Hewitt's mythology actually meant in terms of his own life, art, and times awaits the critical biographer. In the interim, *Ancestral Voices* restates the importance of Hewitt to all the people of whom he came and carries his emphatic rebuke to those who see themselves as pawns in an inevitable historical process:

> We have had enough of the rigid clichés of stubborn politicians, the profit-focused intensity of men of business, the dogmatic arrogance of the Churches, the intolerance of sectarians, the lack of human sympathy of the doctrinaire, of all those whose ready instinct is for violence in word and act.[19]

And, perhaps, this is where the trouble starts – in the divergent and contradictory Irish senses of being a citizen or, more directly, of the definition of *civic space* to which individuals are responsible, beyond immediate demands of home, family, and religion.

In his fine novel *The Death of Men*, set in Italy during the abduction and assassination of Aldo Moro, the Scottish writer Allan Massie has his chief character, Raimundo, remark: 'When l thought about it [a hanging] the rough Justice of the Partisans had done nothing to prepare Italians for civil life: if we contrived to tear ourselves apart, wasn't it to some extent at

---

17 Tom Clyde, Introduction, *Ancestral Voices*, vii.
18 Robert Lowell, *Collected Prose* (London: Faber and Faber, 1987), 263.
19 Hewitt, *Ancestral Voices: The Selected Prose of John Hewitt*, ed. Tom Clyde, 156.

least because of the honour we accorded to that violence we had decided to commemorate.'[20]

Irish life is similarly afflicted – 'the honour we accorded to that violence we had decided to commemorate'. Behind the influential, prim decorum of English law, the northern Unionists, for instance, were willing and able to maintain a little feudal state of their own, self-righteously convinced that their masters in London had been more than well paid, from the rows of ships that slid off the slipways to the dutiful generations that fought the wars and died in their thousands. Now, of course, all that is changed, as indeed it had to, since the North was built as a state upon such precarious foundations. It is grimly tragic, though, that it took so long to recognize this.

While the Republic mesmerizes itself with a postindustrial boom based upon foreign capital and international financial services, the currents of change, north and south, will finally begin to surface and find their own level. As Raimundo remarks:

> It is the State, not the family, which exists as the means of guarding civil life; and that is, after all, what we mean by civilization. It is a product of the State. Without the sanction of the State, we are back in the days of the robber barons. Isn't this what Aquinas meant by his justification of the State, that, for fallen man, it is the *sine qua non* of civil life?[21]

So much writing about life in Ireland and so many lives of Irish writers, in this as in previous generations, has been haunted by that very question.

[1987–1989]

---

20   Allan Massie, *The Death of Men* (London: The Bodley Head, 1981), 240.
21   Massie, 164.

CHAPTER 4

A Question of Imagination

I

My main concern here is with the public face of poetry in Ireland. I hope to show how a poet's identity as a poet is influenced by several literary, cultural, and social assumptions about what poetry is and what 'being a poet' means.

I am mindful of the dangers in approaching my subject in this way – the poem can evaporate into an abstract 'Poetry', and there is also the pitfall to which the Russian poet and critic Osip Mandelstam referred in his essay of 1922, 'On the Nature of the Word':

> If one listens to literary historians who defend evolutionism, it would appear that writers only think about how to clear the road for their successors, but never about how to accomplish their own tasks; or it would appear that they are all participants in an inventor's competition for the improvement of some literary machine, although none of them knows the whereabouts of the judges or what purposes the machine serves.[1]

One needs to be wary of this 'theory', which Mandelstam justifiably calls 'the crudest, most repugnant form of academic ignorance'. This is how he describes its failure:

> In literature nothing is ever 'better', no progress can be made simply because there is no literary machine and no finish line toward which everyone must race as rapidly as possible. This meaningless theory of improvement is not even applicable to the

---

1 Osip Mandelstam, *The Complete Critical Prose and Letters*, ed. J. G. Harris (Ann Arbor, MI: Ardis, 1979), 119.

style and form of the individual writer, for here as well, each gain is accompanied by a loss or forfeit.

So while there is, as Mandelstam maintains, no inevitable progress in literature, it is fair to say that various conventions and pressures can get in the way, restricting and weakening the integrity of poets and poetry to accomplish their fullest potential. I would like to concentrate upon one of these factors: the thematic bias of much contemporary poetry in Ireland.

What I mean by thematic bias are those clichés of history through which poetry is both written and read. The persistent concern with 'identity', for instance, strikes me as being most characteristic of the recent period; of brooding upon what 'Irishness' means and what it is not. Poetry is taken as a central means towards negotiating this definition in, for example, its celebration of Irish landscape, or in the conveyance of that landscape through the Irish language into the poetic forms of English. Uniting both points is the pervasive assumption that history is a terrible home for all Irish poets, the nightmare from which they must escape, like the archetypal artist-figure Stephen Dedalus. Feeding into this convention are various influences, one of the most important of which is that we have a *naturally* poetic language because of the once central influence of the Irish language upon English as it is spoken in the country outside Dublin. While this may well be true in regard to common speech, it is essential to state the obvious here: that whatever benefits a poet can make out of this rich linguistic resource, they will not amount to much unless the poet possesses the necessarily imaginative rigor to *use* them effectively.

Flannery O'Connor's remarks are appropriate here; she addressed a Southern American Writers' Conference on 'the gifts of the region' – speech, contrast, irony, and contradiction:

> … you [may] have seen these gifts abused so often that you have become self-conscious about using them. There is nothing worse than the writer who doesn't use the gifts of the region, but wallows in them.[2]

---

2   Flannery O'Connor, 'Writing Short Stories,' *Mystery and Manners: Occasional Prose* (London: Faber and Faber, 1972), 104.

In Ireland it is possible to relate this question to the way in which 'poetic' language is itself seen as a natural refuge, or home place, for the poet. Language becomes a message from history that the poet receives and transcribes through the medium of vowel, consonant, and assonance as in Seamus Heaney's 'Gifts of Rain: IV': 'The tawny guttural water/ spells itself: Moyola/ is its own score and consort,/ bedding the locale,/ in the utterance,/reed music, an old chanter/breathing its mists/through vowels and history.'[3]

The colloquialism of idiom and image becomes an eloquent defining point of the poetry. The pivotal metaphorical figure is in a place-name (Moyola) and, clustered around it, the images gather from nature (the river), its voice (reed music), and the traditional Irish musical instrument (the Uilean pipes) into a summarizing of 'vowels and history' and the completion of 'pleasure' for the rich man, Dives, 'hoarder of common ground'. These ciphers of meaning become rhetorical and the sentiment conventional in the hands of lesser poets than Seamus Heaney. Literary precedence can be found, as Daniel Hoffman has remarked, in Yeats and latter-day Romanticism where

> ... local-color writing celebrated the individualities of particular places, and gloried in whatever dialectical speech or surviving antiquities of custom or belief could be offered to prove the uniqueness of life in a given locality. Such a course, while risking quaintness, could put into a writer's hands ancient traditions as yet untouched by the mechanical forces of change since the Industrial Revolution. But in Ireland the impetus towards the literary uses of such material was not only from Romantic nostalgia. From the beginnings, the local-color movement had an overt political significance.[4]

The present risk is thematic predictability, with the result that the poetry loses out to a liturgical nostalgia that in the end serves 'political significance'.[5] People and their physical environments recede into the folklore

---

3   Seamus Heaney, 'Gifts of Rain: IV', *Wintering Out* (London: Faber and Faber, 1972), 25.
4   Daniel Hoffman, *Barbarous Knowledge: Myth in the Poetry of Yeats, Graves and Muir* (London: Oxford University Press, 1970), 21.
5   Cf. Raymond Williams's remark, 'Nostalgia, it can be said, is universal and persistent: only other men's nostalgias offend,' in *The Country and the City* (London: Paladin, 1975), 21.

of locale and place-names. Or to paraphrase the German poet Heinrich Heine, poetry is lost in 'green lies', susceptible to the 'fake greenishness' of landscape poetry.[6]

In a review of new poetry in the English literary magazine *Stand*, Terry Eagleton referred to the 'paradigm poem', which 'trades entirely on the intrinsic interest of its materials rather than on any imaginative transformation it submits them to. It is sentimentalism to believe that memories are valuable in themselves. To the writer of regional memories it is often enough a way of evading struggle with meaning, for such lovingly preserved experiences seem deceptively meaningful in themselves, and the act of narrating them assumes an auratic significance for which it has not sufficiently paid'.[7]

The significance that Eagleton is scrutinizing here, in Paul Muldoon's *Quoof*, comes from an assumption that 'the close rendering of an experience is somehow *inherently* meaningful; and this assumption survives only because the urban English reader will tend to collude with it, believing that an experience remote from him/herself – milking a cow, confronting the B-specials – is somehow more inherently significant than one more routinely familiar'. Eagleton approaches this relationship of experience and language from another angle when he writes in *Literary Theory: An Introduction* that if we

> … understand the 'intentions' of a piece of language, we interpret it as being in some sense oriented, structured to achieve certain effects; and none of this can be grasped apart from the practical conditions in which the language operates. It is to see language as practice rather than as object; and there are of course no practices without human subjects.[8]

This is a most convincing argument and, when applied to Irish poetry, it is interesting to note that one of the more discernible trends is away

---

6   Heinrich Heine, *Die Bader von Lucca*, in *H. H. Samtliche Werke*, ed. Hans Kaufman (Munich: Kindler Verlag, 1964), Vol. V, 234–44. I am indebted to Prof. Eoin Bourke, National University of Ireland, Galway for this reference.
7   Terry Eagleton, 'New Poetry,' *Stand Magazine*, 25, No. 3 (Summer 1984), 76–80.
8   Terry Eagleton, *Literary Theory: An Introduction* (Oxford: Basil Blackwell, 1983), 114.

from the use of language as practice towards viewing language in a static sense, as a sacred object. The poet communes with and through language to form an abstract and rhetorical recognition out of his/her own poetic consciousness. It is in Tom Paulin's 'voicing the word *nation*':

> I'm tense now: talk of sharing power,
> prophecies of civil war,
> new reasons for a secular
> mode of voicing the word *nation*
> set us on edge, this generation [.] [9]

It is in John Montague's naming of places: Beragh, Carrickmore, Pomeroy, Fintona –

> placenames that sigh
> like a pressed melodeon
> across this forgotten
> Northern landscape.[10]

Seamus Heaney's work is generally acknowledged for the exemplary nature of precisely this kind of poetic consciousness. Take 'Anahorish', for example, 'soft gradient/ of consonant, vowel-meadow':

> after-image of lamps
> swung through the yards
> on winter evenings.
> With pails and barrows
>
> those mound-dwellers
> go waist-deep in mist
> to break the light ice
> at wells and dunghills.[11]

---

9   Tom Paulin, 'A Nation, Yet Again,' *Liberty Tree* (London: Faber and Faber, 1983), 45.
10 John Montague, 'Last Journey,' *The Dead Kingdom* (Belfast: Blackstaff Press; Dublin: Dolmen Press, 1984), 74–75.
11 Seamus Heaney, 'Anahorish,' *Wintering Out*, 16.

This is a perfect illustration of the way *one* central theme in Heaney's poetry marks out language as an object and of how the poet defines his self and his past in that special pastoral awareness of his own place through a metaphorical appropriation of its idiom.[12] Heaney's *Station Island* shifts this preoccupation on to those occasions, real and imagined, when the poet succumbs to the poetry-making, as he states in 'The Loaning', 'I knew / I was in the limbo of lost words',[13] or in 'Making Strange': 'I found myself driving the stranger'

> through my own country, adept
> at dialect, reciting my pride
> in all that I knew, that began to make strange
> at that same recitation.[14]

Heaney's poems consolidate this process of treating language as an object in that he considers his relation to the very experiences he is writing about *as a poet*. The sequence 'Station Island' seeks to sort out an appropriate place for the poet – one that is adequate to both the world he presently inhabits and the world of his past. My own reading of *Station Island* is that the book represents this particular poetic self-consciousness as confining. It makes Heaney concentrate much more upon the fact that he is writing, as opposed to what he is actually writing about. Perhaps this is the likely result if we bear in mind the perspective that Terry Eagleton offers in the above quotations. For if language becomes an object in the poet's hands, the occasion of his writing will be viewed with equal importance, and by its very literariness this focuses on the poet and the personality of his or her own artistic self in relaying the poem to us: 'Then I sat there writing, imagining in silence/sounds like love sounds after long abstinence',

> Now I sit blank as gradual morning brightens
> its distancing, inviolate expanse.[15]

---

12   A useful comparison can be made with Derek Walcott's *Midsummer* (London: Faber and Faber, 1984).
13   Seamus Heaney, *Station Island* (London: Faber and Faber, 1984).
14   Heaney, *Station Island*, 32–33.
15   Heaney, *Station Island*, 24.

Much attention to Irish poetry is centred on these themes. The critical perspectives converge upon where the poet fits into public debate (Paulin's 'prophecies of civil war'), the delineation of nostalgic landscapes of home (Montague's 'small hills & hidden villages') and the sense of being a poet in the first place (Heaney's 'I sat there writing, imagining in silence').

In Ireland, too, there is a widely held perception of the poet as some kind of public figure who, in regard to both his social life and beliefs, voices on behalf of 'the people' an accessible articulation of their spiritual and cultural beliefs. This stereotypical image of the poet as a public figure is possibly derived from the populist context in which Irish poetry in English developed, from the mid-nineteenth to the early part of the twentieth century. However, the fact there are now dramatically changed social and cultural conditions, wherein complex and contradictory ideals conflict, does not seem to have substantially altered this perception of the poet. It may well be another remnant of that Romantic idealism to which Daniel Hoffman refers; in this instance, of seeing the poet as a sensitive soul, damaged at birth by a fragmented inheritance, bearing artistically the scars of a repressed Irish cultural milieu. A failure, in other words, not of our own making, but of England's; their language, imposed on ours; their culture forced upon us.

This conventional and normative view still obtains in Ireland, and poetry internalizes the vision, transforming it into an acceptable myth that sustains the generally accepted cultural and politico-religious dogmas.[16] As Seán O'Faoláin remarked in *The Irish*, Irish writers from about '1890 to about 1940 … saw Irish life, in the main, romantically. It was as a poetic people that they first introduced themselves to the world, and it is as a poetic people that they are still mainly known abroad.'[17]

16 I looked at this viewpoint elsewhere: 'A Question of Covenants; Modern Irish Poetry,' *The Crane Bag*, 3, No. 2 (1979); 'Checkpoints: The Younger Irish Poets,' *The Crane Bag*, 6, No. 1 (1982); 'Convention as Conservatism,' *The Crane Bag*, 7, No. 2 (1984); 'Poetry and the Public: Solitude and Participation,' *The Crane Bag*, 8, No. 2 (1984); and 'The Permanent City: The Younger Irish Poets' in *The Irish Writer and the City*, ed. Maurice Harmon (Gerrards Cross: Colin Smythe; Totowa, New Jersey: Barnes & Noble, 1984), 180–90.
17 Seán O'Faoláin, *The Irish* (Harmondsworth, Middlesex: Penguin Books, 1969), (Har

Poetry itself continues to be seen in this light, both in Ireland and elsewhere, as not so much imaginatively *questioning* reality, but rather in *naturalizing* the traditional and inherited ways of reading it. This attitude may well come from the political nature of Irish life where a homogeneous cultural nationalism holds sway and is to be mediated through the established images and modes of writing.

It is noticeable then that, given the crisis-prone history of present-day Ireland, with its proverbial emphasis on 'identity', traditional roles have asserted themselves in the poet's own work and the audience's expectations of that work. This conformity is an illustration of how generally acceptable that tradition is to poets. An artistic need to challenge it often occurs in poets who endeavour to examine those aspects of freedom (personal as much as social) that are available to them in the context of the literary and historical conditions of modern Ireland. Thomas Kinsella's 1966 address to the Modern Language Association in New York, he stated: 'It is not as though literature, or national life, were a corporate, national investigation of a corporate national experience – as though a nation were a single animal, with one complex artistic feeler.'[18]

In articulating this basic 'fact', Kinsella also picked out the essential condition of any poet writing today:

> … every writer in the modern world – since he can't be in all the literary traditions at once – is the inheritor of a gapped, discontinuous, polyglot tradition. Nevertheless, if the function of tradition is to link us living with the significant past, this is done as well by a broken tradition as by a whole one.

It is the imaginative exploration of this condition, of a 'broken tradition', that distinguishes the best of Kinsella's poems, as it does the poetry of Derek Mahon. His poetry, it can be said, composes that 'gapped, discontinuous, polyglot tradition' to which Kinsella alludes. For Mahon brings into creative alignment with our own time a whole range of writers from Brecht and Pasternak to Gérard de Nerval, and his particular accomplishment has been the way he has discovered a *poetic* voice to achieve these

---

18   Thomas Kinsella, 'The Irish Writer' in *Davis, Mangan, Ferguson? Tradition and the Irish Writer* (Dublin: Dolmen Press, 1970), 66.

new imaginative perspectives. It is a poetry of manner, highly tense yet balanced, and formally set within the conditions of definite times and places, but ineluctably leading out of these to wider questions, thoughts, and feelings. By its very composure, Mahon's austerity of language rebukes sentimentality and denies any appeal to rhetoric. This incontrovertible restraint energizes the poetry, drawing its forcefulness from the poet speaking his mind:

> When I returned one year ago
> I felt like Tonio Kröger – slow
> To come to terms with my own past
> Yet knowing I could never cast
> Aside the things that made me what,
> For better or worse, I am.[19]

Feelings here are held in reserve, as a private matter mostly, but the actual world, which is being scrutinized in a dynamic way, includes the poet's sense of himself. This form of imaginative address can, in turn, be contrasted with the substantive formal disintegration one finds in the poetry of Padraic Fiacc.[20] Ironically, at a time when extensive discussion surrounds Irish literature, of how it relates to history and how the present crises have challenged the poet's imagination, Fiacc is rarely mentioned. Yet his work, on every conceivable artistic level of style and content, records the collapse of a society, its past, and the nature of its contradictory ideals. Perhaps one reason for this failure of criticism relates to the kind of traditional relationship that exists between an Irish (or British) poet and his audience. Fiacc's poetry mocks this relationship and brings seriously into question the poet's place as regards a society (like Northern Ireland's) that lurches from crisis to crisis. It is a poetry that has little in common with the well-intentioned decorum that underlies the following

---

19   Derek Mahon, 'The Sea in Winter,' *Poems 1962–1978* (London: Oxford University Press, 1979), 111.
20   Padraic Fiacc's books include: *By the Black Stream: Selected Poems 1947–1967* (Dublin: Dolmen Press, 1969); *Odour of Blood* (Newbridge, Co. Kildare: The Goldsmith Press, 1973, rep. 1984); *Nights in the Bad Place* (Belfast: Blackstaff Press, 1977); *The Selected Padraic Fiacc* (Belfast: Blackstaff Press, 1979).

comment from the introduction to *The Penguin Book of Contemporary British Poetry*:

> It is interesting to speculate on the relationship between the resurgence of Northern Irish writing and the Troubles. The poets have all experienced a sense of 'living in important places' and have been under considerable pressure to 'respond'. They have been brought hard up against questions about the relationship between art and politics, between the private and the public, between conscious 'making' and intuitive 'inspiration'. But on the whole they have avoided a poetry of directly documentary reportage.[21]

Speculations apart, Fiacc's poems have, for the past three decades, carried the marks of disaffection, prejudice, and hope that are embedded in ordinary northern Irish speech and idiom, and have formally and experimentally balanced the conscious 'making', the intuitive 'inspiration' *with* a poetry of 'directly documentary reportage'. Perhaps Fiacc's position is explicable in similar terms to Raymond Williams's remark that Thomas Hardy was 'very disturbing for someone trying to rationalise refined, civilised, balancing judgment. Hardy exposes so much that cannot be displaced from its social situation, particularly in the later books.'[22] Indeed Fiacc's later work, in particular, sympathetically and critically explores the social, cultural, and religious situation and the illusions fostered by both sides in the northern conflict. This makes an exceptional witness out of his poetry, rather than making it a testament to 'living in important places'.[23] His poetry is important precisely because it *revokes* those very notions and

---

21 *The Penguin Book of Contemporary British Poetry*, eds. Blake Morrison and Andrew Motion (Harmondsworth, Middlesex: Penguin Books, 1982), 16.
22 Raymond Williams, *Politics and Letters: Interviews with New Left Review* (London: N.L.B. Verso ed., 1981), 246.
23 Damian Gorman remarks on this matter: '… part of the reason why so many of our local poets are so well known across the water is that this is a troubled region, deserving media attention. Thus poets are to some degree indebted to the situation. Our most urgent trouble at present is a complete lack of political imagination. It seems to me that men and women of poetic imagination might make a greater contribution to those reserves of communality which will be needed to spirit us out of a state of attrition.' 'Does Poetry Matter in Northern Ireland?' *Fortnight: An Independent Review for Northern Ireland*, No. 217 (April, 1985), 19.

assumptions that I have looked at earlier in this essay by subverting them and leaving in their place little by way of *traditional* aesthetic consolation. Instead, we find a harrowing act of imaginative redemption or an image bordering on what is grotesquely, comically human. Fiacc's poem 'The Wearing of the Black', for instance, mediates between the formal family scene of himself as a boy, 'like the Prince of Wales', listening to his mother playing the piano, and the knowledgeable background of his father '*gone to America for / He is on the bloody run!*' The recollected music of 'See the Conquering Hero Comes' and 'The Bluebells of Scotland' gives way as the awkward young boy drops a porcelain teacup:

> Now, half a century after, why
> Can I recall that flash of fire on the tile
> Floor as I scalded my bare knees when I pray
> To care even that this rotting self-dinner-
> jacketed hero's grave, tonight, in black cuff
>
> Links at least has the wit to dress for death.[24]

The clash between these two worlds of the past and present is characteristic of Fiacc's poetry, as is the culminating wry portrait that links both worlds in a new and disturbing perspective. It is as if nothing ever changes, only our ability to remember. The 'political situation' as Milan Kundera remarks, 'has brutally illuminated the ordinary metaphysical problem of forgetting that we face all the time, every day, without paying any attention. Politics unmasks the metaphysics of private life, private life unmasks the metaphysics of politics.'[25] Possibly another reason for Fiacc's neglect is that his poetry unceasingly reasserts the unpalatable truthfulness of Kundera's statement. Indeed there is a 'political' consciousness in Fiacc's poetry, an appropriate rhetoric that brings his work much closer to European and American models than it is to English poetry. This only further underlines his comparative isolation as a strangely modernistic

---

24   Padraic Fiacc, *Nights in the Bad Place*, 37.
25   Milan Kundera, 'Afterword: A Talk with the Author by Philip Roth,' *The Book of Laughter and Forgetting* (Harmondsworth, Middlesex: Penguin Books, 1983), 235.

voice while he completes his 'Missa Terribilis', in the form of a traditional Mass.²⁶

The poetry of Padraic Fiacc, Thomas Kinsella, and Derek Mahon, as well as that of some of their younger contemporaries such as Paul Durcan, demonstrates a relative freedom from the kind of public conformations and conventions that I have noted briefly in the poetry of Montague, Heaney, and Paulin. The poetic fruits of this freedom are found in the poet's own ironic, critical, and questioning relationship with the details of his individual experience, feelings, and ideas, and of how rigorously these are probed in and through the poetry. This is a valuable, if sometimes obscured, development: an imaginative negotiation that takes into account the Ireland we actually live in and the image poetry presents of it, along with all the other things that a poet might imagine.

[1988]

---

26   Padraic Fiacc, 'Missa Terribilis: A Sequence,' *Paris/Atlantic; An Irish Issue* (American College in Paris, Paris, Summer 1985), subsequently collected in *Missa Terribilis* (Belfast: Blackstaff Press, 1986).

CHAPTER 5

How's the Poetry Going?

I

Sometime back at a reception for the announcement of literary awards for young and promising new writers, mostly attended by PR people and the sponsors, a well-known academic and writer came up to me. After exchanging a few brief pleasantries (who is ever really relaxed at such gatherings?) he left on the words, 'And how's the poetry going?' I knew he meant well and it was, after all, only an attempt at concerned familiarity, a little like saying, 'Has the bad leg healed yet?' The phrase struck me though, suggesting something that I would like to explore here, if a little hesitantly: the nature of the Irish literary community. I say hesitantly because I am well aware of the pitfalls that lie ahead. Whether you like it or not, to turn your attention to the community, large or small, in which you live and work can be a dangerous business. It is all very well to question and probe those of others, but when did we last see or hear of politicians questioning their own structures and ambitions; or the media in Ireland examining their own nature and objectives; or arts administrators and promoters asking, beyond the rhetoric, what their function actually is in Irish society today?

My own experience is limited to particular prejudices, the most adamant of which is a constitutional antipathy to cliques or groups of one kind or another. I have always believed that writers, painters, sculptors, all artists need independence and the more mature the culture they come from, the more that independence is guaranteed through schooling and the media. This is not to say that I think writers should exist in glorious isolation; far from it. The civic world, social space, is there to be enjoyed as best it can by all and sundry, irrespective of their work. Political responsibilities or commitments are exercised, rejected, or ignored by each individual citizen and this includes the writer, of course, who is no different on this score at least.

What concerns me here is the centripetal force that compels writers in Ireland to share basic ideas, ideals, and ambitions (a common understanding) on fundamental politico-cultural levels: the assumption that we all are, really, one big (though maybe not all the time, happy) family.

In recent years it has become a *vogue* for writers to describe themselves as 'full-time writers', as if, like footballers, there are semi-professionals who only play at weekends and hold on to the day job as well. As someone who has lived precariously enough, balanced between writing and teaching after a short spell as a librarian, to emerge in his late thirties as a writer, I have realized how some office-bound administrators, like T. S. Eliot and Wallace Stevens, librarians like Philip Larkin, secretaries like Stevie Smith, diplomats like Denis Devlin, mothers like Sylvia Plath, and doctors like William Carlos Williams, have all devoted their lives to writing in a manner that defies the comfortingly self-regarding phrase of 'full-time writer'. Nadine Gordimer scotched this idea in 'A Bolter and the Invincible Summer':

> I'm not flattered by the idea of being presented with a 'profession', *honoris causa;* every honest writer or painter wants to achieve the impossible and needs no minimum standard laid down by an establishment such as a profession.[1]

Yet regularly in Ireland writers are described as 'professional' and some, no doubt, take comfort from the fact, particularly when the 'establishment' that offers the description happens to be the media. And, flowing from this anxiety, there seems to be a need amongst the writing community for approval. This is a curious dilemma. Irish writers, surprisingly too the 'young' and the 'promising' as much as the 'well known' and the 'established', have an ambiguous and unresolved tension between themselves and the public world of recognition that exists around them.

As Dennis O'Driscoll pointed out with characteristic verve:

---

[1] Nadine Gordimer, 'A Bolter and the Invincible Summer', *The Essential Gesture: Writing, Politics and Places* (London: Jonathan Cape, 1988), 19.

> The problem, actually, is not that the Irish Republic can be too difficult a place to establish a reputation as a poet but that it may be too easy…. Those with more tenacity than talent will find magazines to publish them, radio slots to broadcast their 'thoughts for the day', arts centres to host their readings, newspapers to publicise their activities…. As I know to my cost, Irish poets are apt to take grave offence at adverse criticism, however mild and well-meant. As a result many discriminating critics gradually eschew the reviewing of local produce altogether, resulting in a dearth of authoritative and independent reviewing. An indifference towards standards is particularly evident in those sections of the media which are willing to yield air space and column inches to self-proclaimed poets on the basis that if you declare yourself to be a poet, you must be a poet; if you declare it often enough and loudly enough, you must be a 'leading' poet.[2]

This urge (to 'declare yourself to be a poet') is so much more to do with recognition than with the rigors of art. And, as Dennis O'Driscoll candidly reminds us, 'indifference towards standards' refers in effect to those channels, forms of attention, that are readily, indeed eagerly, accepted in Ireland whereby the poet and the putative reader *know* each other and register that a poem has taken place. It is a code-sign under which, all too often, the poet gives what is expected while the discipline of art, that essential gesture, becomes secondary to the business of being a poet.

It is worthwhile taking a little time to ponder this business. Historically, we can track the available images in Ireland of what the artist is via the dominant presence of Joyce, since in comparison to Yeats, his influence has been the greater because longer-lasting *inside* the country. As Richard Ellmann points out, with *A Portrait of the Artist as a Young Man* completed, Joyce 'had pretty well exhausted the possibilities of the artist-hero'. Discussing Ibsen with his brother, Stanislaus, in 1907, Joyce remarks:

> Life is not so simple as Ibsen represents it. Mrs Alving, for instance, is Motherhood and so on…. It's all very fine and large, of course. If it had been written at the time of Moses, we'd now think it wonderful. But it had no importance at this age of the world. It is a remnant of heroics too.[3]

---

2 Dennis O'Driscoll, 'Irish Roundup,' *Poetry Review,* Vol. 79, No. 1, (1989), 38–40.
3 Richard Ellmann, *Four Dubliners: Wilde, Yeats, Joyce and Beckett* (London: Hamish Hamilton, 1987), 71.

Then, in conclusion, Ellmann summarizes Joyce's accomplishment as an artist very much opposed to heroics:

> He objected to slavishness and ignobility; he thought they were fostered by conventional notions of heroism, which turned men and women into effigies. He wished them to know themselves as they really were, not as they were taught by church and state to consider themselves to be. He gave dignity to the common life that we all share.[4]

It is this antiheroic side of Joyce that we seem to have lost sight of in favour of the Poet as Hero; a view sanctioned by Irish political history seen from a nationalist perspective. But one cannot be anything but deeply saddened by the legacy of this myth: the endless stream of Behan 'stories', the one about Paddy Kavanagh, what happened to poor Myles the night … as these men are reduced to actual illness, alcoholism, irrelevant squabbles, vendettas, and premature graves: Behan died at 40, Flann O'Brien at 55, and Kavanagh at 63. 'Mighty characters': how often has that phrase been used patronizingly of Irish writers?

Since his death in 1967, things have changed, but, as Kavanagh himself well knew, changes can often be mere window dressing. In his *Self-Portrait* he remarks:

> I realise it would not have been easy for a man of sensibility to survive in the society of my birth, but it could have been done had I been trained in the technique of reserve and restraint. A poet is never one of the people. He is detached, remote, and the life of small-time dances and talk about football would not be for him. He might take part but could not belong.[5]

This is Kavanagh speaking: the poet many see as being quintessentially *of* the people; applauded and held up as an example of the 'true' bardic Irish tradition. For Kavanagh, 'the real problem' is 'the scarcity of a right audience which draws out of a poet what is best in him. The Irish audience that I came into contact with tried to draw out of me everything that was loud, journalistic and untrue.' In perhaps the most damning

---

4   Ellmann, *Four Dubliners: Wilde, Yeats, Joyce and Beckett*, 76.
5   Patrick Kavanagh, *Self-Portrait* (Dublin: The Dolmen Press, 1963), 13–14.

comment of all, Kavanagh declares: 'What the alleged poetry-lover loved was the Irishness of a thing. Irishness is a form of anti-art. A way of posing as a poet without actually being one.' And in the 'Author's Note' to his *Collected Poems*, Kavanagh says: 'I am always shy of calling myself a poet and I wonder much at those young men and sometimes those old men who boldly declare their poeticality. If you ask them what they are, they say: "Poet".'[6] Curious that around the same time, the Italian poet Eugenio Montale should remark: 'It has happened that in the face of the massive production of poems that has invaded our country, and not only ours, I have found the title of "poet" somewhat intolerable.'[7] It is his *resistance* to the demands of the 'loud, journalistic and untrue' that makes Kavanagh so important. As the Australian poet Les Murray remarked:

> ... people who should know better seem to have caved in completely to a journalistic ideal of irresponsible excitement; controversy and ill-will are welcomed as 'lively' and 'controversial' when really they are tragic. They make 'good radio', exciting publicity, but they are a symptom of a deadly sickness in our culture.[8]

We may frown at that phrase 'deadly sickness' but as Murray and Kavanagh know, 'the writer's problems are in some ultimate sense the problems of society'. As Cleanth Brooks has demonstrated in his essay 'The Writer and His Community', for Yeats 'the plight of the poet ... is a kind of measuring stick for the health of the civilization – indeed one of the most important measurements that we have'.[9] So how is it then that, in this most literary of cultures (the Irish), poetry is generally viewed as everything but an *art form*. The truly amazing thing is that this perception has not changed with time. As an indirect result, many writers in this country either left (like Samuel Beckett and Brian Coffey) or else put up

---

6   Patrick Kavanagh, 'Author's Note,' *Collected Poems* (London: MacGibbon & Kee, 1964), xiii.
7   Eugenio Montale, *The Second Life of Art: Selected Essays* (New York: The Ecco Press, 1982), 321.
8   Les Murray, *The Peasant Mandarin* (Queensland: University of Queensland Press, 1978), 259–260.
9   Cleanth Brooks, 'The Modern Writer and His Community,' *A Shaping Joy: Studies in the Writer's Craft* (London: Methuen, 1971), 25.

with the situation and, in the process, damaged themselves, like Patrick Kavanagh. It was Beckett who wrote so dismissively to Thomas MacGreevy in 1938 of his 'chronic inability to understand ... a phrase like "The Irish People" or to imagine it ever gave a fart ... for any form of art, whatsoever, whether before the Union or after'.[10] And Patrick Kavanagh, often seen as the 'traditional' Irish poet in contrast to the 'cosmopolitan' Beckett, could be equally contemptuous of Irish culture in his *Self-Portrait*. Indeed, the poems Kavanagh wrote are shadowed by this awareness as he attempted to find an authentic image for himself as a poet, caught between terrible bouts of self-consciousness and justifiable rage. In doing so, he tried to subvert some of the clichés. Take his poem 'I Had a Future', for example, with its poignant concluding refrain:

> It is summer and the eerie beat
> Of madness in Europe trembles the
> Wings of the butterflies along the canal.
>
> O I had a future.[11]

What comes through much of Kavanagh's poetry is his realization that there was no 'natural community' for him as a poet. He had instead to create a community. But the point is that this challenge is unavoidable for any poet. It is in effect the condition for writing poetry in this day and age. To pretend otherwise, as so often happens in Ireland today, is only to highlight those biases and needs in both the individual poet and the society in which they live and write. Only when poets have separated themselves from the past and its heritage, and transcended it, can they become truly effective and truly themselves as writers. In Ireland this goes against the grain, for our nostalgia insists that we maintain the illusion, at the very least, of being forever of the one place and of the one people. This might partially account for the popularity of Irish literature abroad: a consolation for jaded postmodern palates. To cut across this loyalty, transforming it and making possible a change in consciousness, is seen as some kind of betrayal

10   Deirdre Bair, *Samuel Beckett: A Biography* (London: Jonathan Cape, 1978),. 281.
11   Patrick Kavanagh, 'I Had a Future,' *Selected Poems* (Harmondsworth, Middlesex: Penguin Books, 1996), 104.

or sell-out. As Nadine Gordimer put it, 'loyalty is an emotion, integrity a conviction adhered to out of moral values'. And there is also Beckett's famous *credo*: 'The artist who stakes his being comes from no particular place. And he has no brothers.' But Irish literature is meant to conform to already existent cultural-political mores or 'loyalties', rather than challenging these or inspiring others to do so on the basis of artistic convictions. For, behind the myth itself (and the caricature of poetry that follows close behind), there is often a masked disdain for 'the people', together with an exploitation of – and poetic acquiescence in – their historical condition. Rather than showing possible imaginative ways out of this morass, poets and poetry all too often consort with it.

The bitterness, isolation, and nostalgia that permeate a lot of what Patrick Kavanagh wrote derives from these disillusioned feelings – of his being, in a way, an exile, stranded in the uncaring city and finding a kind of compensatory community for himself with other like-minded people. Yet, as Cleanth Brooks has it, to 'become a member of a literary *clique* or to find oneself the object of a cult of readers and followers is not the same thing as to be part of a community. The *clique* is too close to one's life and perhaps too complacent of one's faults; the cult is too remote and too much given to unthinking adulation.' Kavanagh seems to have hated this business – and who would blame him? Its self-consciousness and claustrophobia must have drained him, as indeed poems like 'Jungle', 'Literary Adventures', and 'The Defeated' suggest. His poetry can be read as being about the imagination separated from the common life of the everyday, of his being cut off from what he called 'the habitual, the banal'. In their rightful place, Kavanagh sees the usurping literary world ganging up on the vital imagination and the true world of the innocent spirit. It is a powerful, redemptive vision, profoundly influential in Ireland since Kavanagh's death, but one that was culturally sapped of energy by the very society Kavanagh sought to indict. Instead, it lapped up the irascible Kavanagh's frustrated outbursts.

What Kavanagh gave vent to was his need as a poet to be part of the community in which he lived: to find or rediscover a common cause and experience with it on *artistic* terms. But, while resisting the sentimental populism of his day, the only option available to him was as the cantankerous rebel: 'a terrible man' – the role Irish society had (and has) absolutely no problem in accepting or, indeed, expecting of its poets. However, there is a distinct unease, when poetry is taken, not frivolously, solemnly, or with morbid introspection, but *seriously*, like any other art form. Nothing more, nothing less.

In 'Epic', one of his best-known and most anthologized poems, Kavanagh recollects 'The Duffys shouting "Damn Your Soul"' and

> … old McCabe stripped to the waist, seen
> Step the plot defying the blue-cast steel –
> 'Here is the march along these iron stones'.[12]

Bertolt Brecht, a slightly older contemporary, was coming to terms with his exile in 'the year of the Munich bother' to which 'Epic' alludes. Which was more important, Kavanagh asks, this or 'the Munich bother'? He answers: 'I inclined / to lose my faith in Ballyrush and Gortin / Till Homer's ghost came whispering to my mind / He said: I made the *Iliad* from such / A local row. Gods make their own importance.'[13] Brecht curiously inverts this reasoning in a poem of 1939 called 'In Dark Times':

> They won't say: when the walnut tree shook in the wind
> But: when the house-painter crushed the workers.
> They won't say: when the child skimmed a flat stone across the rapids
> But: when the great wars are being paid for.
> They won't say: when the woman came into the room
> But: when the great powers joined forces against the workers.
> However, they won't say: the times were dark
> Rather: why were their poets silent.[14]

Later still, Brecht describes his reasons for writing, and the context in which he was to write 'Bad Time for Poetry', where the house-painter again stands for Hitler:

> In my poetry a rhyme
> Would seem to me almost insolent.

---

12 Patrick Kavanagh, 'I Had a Future,' *Selected Poems*, 'Epic,' 101.
13 Kavanagh, 'I Had a Future,' *Selected Poems*, 'Epic,' 101.
14 Bertolt Brecht, 'In Dark Times,' *Bertolt Brecht Poems* (London: Eyre Methuen, 1976), 274.

> Inside me contend
> Delight at the apple tree in blossom
> And horror at the house-painter's speeches.
> But only the second
> Drives me to my desk.[15]

It does not matter whether we agree with Brecht here or not, and whether or not that 'only' is just. The crucial shift has taken place away from the individuality of 'the poet' (and all the old romantic hang-ups and media hype and puff that go along with that outmoded notion) towards sorting out a place for poetry in practice in the world. I think the same can be said for the Russian poets, like Anna Akhmatova, Osip Mandelstam, and Boris Pasternak, not to mention the self-mockeries of Robert Lowell or John Berryman, or the antiheroic poetic of Eugenio Montale.

In a way both Kavanagh and Brecht fought against the orthodoxies and clichés of their own time – one that was stultifying and the other that was literally deadly. While Kavanagh tried to preserve some sort of artistic authenticity in the face of official chauvinistic 'Irishness' and all the other material odds stacked up against him, Brecht was in the United States in 1947 confronting the now notorious Committee on Un-American Activities. In a masterly display, he turned the tables against his bland accusers by equating Hitler's attacks on 'un-German activities' with their 'un-American' witch hunt:

> I wish to say that the great American people would lose much and risk much if they allowed anybody to restrict free competition of ideas in cultural fields, or to interfere with art, which must be free in order to be art.[16]

As Brecht knew, the assumptions that gave rise to the Committee are never too far from the surface in any culture that restricts, out of fear, doctrine, or expediency, what he called 'the free competition of ideas in cultural fields'. Without that real, or, more often than not, imagined freedom poets run the risk of being the playthings of their own delusions of power.

[1990]

---

15 Brecht, 'Bad Time for Poetry,' *Bertolt Brecht Poems*, 330–31.
16 Brecht, 30 October 1947.

CHAPTER 6

Invocation of Powers: John Montague

I

In the title essay of his collection, *The Figure in the Cave and Other Essays*, John Montague reveals the extent to which his adult life and work have been directed towards creating for himself a central place in the Irish literary canon.[1] It is an ambition, as the essay outlines, deeply influenced by the experiences Montague underwent as a child, first uprooted from his family in New York, and subsequently returned to Northern Ireland as a foster child in the care of elderly aunts in County Tyrone. The sense of dislocation that pervades Montague's poetry, and the self-conscious search for both a real (emotional) and imagined (cultural) home represent the twin matters that I want to discuss here. In John Montague's poetry the bond between these preoccupations proves to be the presentation of his own 'self' as it responds to, and anticipates, various elements in Irish literary and political history. The essay to which I have referred is important in this particular regard for, as his editor, Antoinette Quinn, has pointed out, Montague is 'primarily an autobiographical poet for whom the provincial and local unrest and violence, whether historical or contemporary, are extensions of ancestral, familial and personal traumas'.[2]

---

1   John Montague, *The Figure in the Cave and Other Essays* (Dublin: The Lilliput Press, 1989).
2   Antoinette Quinn, 'The Well-Beloved: Montague and the Muse,' in *Irish University Review*, 19, 1 (Spring, 1989). This essay elaborates upon these themes, in particular Montague's sense of being 'a virtual orphan ... continually seeking to compensate for the maternal bonding of which he was deprived in infancy.' The present writer will not pursue the psychological dimensions of such a quest, but rather concentrate upon the nature of their transformation into art.

In 'The Figure in the Cave', Montague relates his personal life story to his artistic life. At several points they intersect and take on an historical significance of self-mythologizing:

> ... Brooklyn-born, Tyrone-reared, Dublin-educated, constituted a tangle, a turmoil of contradictory allegiance it would take a lifetime to unravel. And the chaos within contrasted with the false calm without: Ireland, both North and South, then seemed to me 'a fen of stagnant waters'. And there was no tradition for someone of my background to work in; except for the ahistorical genius of Kavanagh.... I am not only joking, for, hard as it may be to understand today, there was no Northern dimension to Irish literature then.[3]

The 'then' is the late 1950s and early 1960s. What Montague clearly seeks to establish here is his own place in Irish literature, notwithstanding the 'ahistorical genius of Kavanagh'. Throughout the essay, Montague informs us of the role he played in restoring to print such poets as John Hewitt and Patrick Kavanagh, how he simultaneously promoted the notion of what he calls 'the French idea of a fertile literary community' since he 'would not wish anyone to go through what [he] endured as a young writer'.[4] Montague goes on to list his work in this regard: *The Dolmen Miscellany of Irish Writing* (1961), *The Faber Book of Irish Verse* (1974), and *Bitter Harvest* (1989).[5]

Having therefore outlined his making available a tradition that was either historical (the Gaelic poets of the eighteenth century) or otherwise obscured (like Kavanagh or Hewitt), Montague traces the wider net of his ambition by revealing his 'veneration for older writers of genius' such as Ezra Pound, Wallace Stevens, Hugh MacDiarmid, David Jones, Samuel Beckett, Austin Clarke, and Robert Graves:

---

3   Montague, *The Figure in the Cave*, 8–9. The blurb on the cover of Montague's collection *Mount Eagle* (Meath: The Gallery Press, 1988) states: 'John Montague commands a pivotal place in contemporary Irish writing. His achievement ... may be seen as a vital link between Patrick Kavanagh's instruction and a number of important younger poets.'
4   Montague, *The Figure in the Cave*, 'I was editing the poetry of Patrick Kavanagh in the background ...,' 10; 'In helping to get Kavanagh and Hewitt back into print,' 15.
5   Montague, *The Figure in the Cave*, 15.

> Graves was also writing in a tradition of love poetry going back to the *amour courtois* which began ... in the valley of the Dordogne, a tradition in which I also inscribe myself, with modern hesitations. But I was always fond of my literary fathers, in verse and prose, and they usually returned the compliment.[6]

As earlier in the essay, when Montague writes of his own name and its changing from Tague to Montague ('I have played upon our change of name and am delighted that in the original Irish *taidgh* means "son of the philosopher, poet or fool": I claim all three'), the important point is the identification with other writers as 'my literary fathers' and the sense of approval-seeking.[7] This form of self-vindication is furthered by the preoccupied manner in which Montague relates himself to 'several interlocking groups of writers' outside Ireland, from Gary Snyder, Robert Duncan, Charles Tomlinson, and Ted Hughes, to poets writing in languages other than English, such as Octavio Paz. The tradition-making that such listing implies bears down directly upon one of the concluding motifs from 'The Figure in the Cave' as essay and as collection.

Montague meditates on the way 'destiny seems to have decided to give me back my lost childhood in America' with the honour of a first US honorary doctorate and a reception from both houses of the New York legislature while 'my Tyrone background is being destroyed by bulldozer and bomb. Ballygawley is now as black a name as the South Bronx or Brooklyn':

> It is like a fairytale, the little child who was sent away being received back with open arms. But while awed at the reappearance of this golden cradle to rock my dotage, I am grateful to have explored Ireland so intimately. Standing-stones and streams are not part of Brooklyn nor are *cailleachs*. To judge by my contemporaries I would probably have been a writer, certainly a journalist, had I stayed in America. But who cut the long wound of poetry into my youth? Was it my mother who chose for her own good reasons to cast me off?[8]

---

6   Montague, *The Figure in the Cave*. It is interesting to note Montague's 'Introduction' to *Poisoned Lands* (new ed. Dublin: Dolmen Press, 1977): 'An editor-poet I studiously avoided was T. S. Eliot but when the volume was being considered for American publication, it crossed his desk. Old Possum risked a friendly pat: 'I have, indeed, found Mr Montague's poems worthy of study', 10.
7   Montague, *The Figure in the Cave*, 11.
8   Montague, *The Figure in the Cave*, 17–18.

II

John Montague has published ten collections of poetry between *Forms of Exile* (1958) and *Mount Eagle* (1988). Alongside these volumes, two works of fiction have appeared: *Death of a Chieftain* (1964) and *The Lost Notebook* (1988). I will focus here upon a cluster of poems that act as an imaginative counterweight to my introduction.

In the previous quotation from 'The Figure in the Cave' Montague directly associated poetry with 'the long wound' and his sense of being 'cast off'. Poetry is both an affliction and, by implication, a mode of consolation and compensation. The individual 'self' is repatriated to the lost homeland through poetry and held up as a focus of (predominantly inherited) social, political, literary, and cultural experiences. The overriding impression this figure presents in Montague's poetry is that of a 'victim'.

There are, for instance, the portraits of womanhood such as the *cailleach* (which is Irish for an old woman, or hag) from 'The Wild Dog Rose'[9] who suffers rape and loneliness, the 'old bitch, with a warm mouthful of game' in 'Dowager',[10] a representative of the Anglo-Irish caste, humming 'with satisfaction in the sun'. More convincingly, there is Nurse Mullen from 'Herbert Street Revisited',[11] who 'knelt by her bedside / to pray for her lost Mayo hills, / the bruised bodies of Easter Volunteers' before her own death, 'upright / in her chair, facing a window / warm with the blue slopes of Nephin'.

The characteristic gesture is passive acceptance: 'treading the pattern / of one time and place into history' as Montague remarks in 'Herbert Street Revisited'. Resignation or acceptance is a typical note in the poetry as memories are fixed upon family items like a locket or a silver flask.[12] In the face of Nature too, the dominant note is elegiac, the landscape

---

9   Montague, *The Rough Field* (Meath: The Gallery Press, 1989), 78–80.
10 Montague, *A Slow Dance* (Dublin: Dolmen Press, 1975), 23.
11 Montague, *The Great Cloak* (Dublin: Dolmen Press, 1978), 40–42.
12 Montague, 'The Locket' and 'The Silver Flask' in *The Dead Kingdom* (Mountrath: Dolmen Press, 1984), 92, 72.

representing 'a manuscript / We had lost the skill to read, / A part of our past disinherited'.[13]

The landscape is charged with historical signs and symbols that the poet decodes as best he can, knowing, all the while, the 'severed head' that 'chokes to / speak another tongue'. So, from figures of the victim, to a sense of resignation and the very 'humiliation' of finding his ancestral language suppressed, the poet seeks an understanding of his own 'speech' in 'The Sound of a Wound': 'Scar tissue/can rend, the old hurt/tear open.'[14] Yet out of this loss, 'the old hurt', Montague summons 'in my bloodstream' bitterness inherited 'from my father, the /swarm of blood/to the brain, the vomit surge/of race hatred,/ the victim seeing the oppressor,/bold Jacobean /planter, or gadget laden marine'. The recurrence of this image of the wound and its association with loss is unmistakable in Montague's poetry. His father, 'a traditional Irishman' in 'The Cage', is reimagined: 'his bald head behind / the bars of the small booth the mark of an old car / accident beating on his / ghostly forehead',[15] while in the uncollected poem, 'Sands', about Bobby Sands, the IRA hunger striker who died, the reconciliation of wound as metaphor with loss is subsumed into the absolute mark of sacrifice as a historical birth right:

> This is a sign of silence.
> This is the sound of the bone
> breaking through skin
> of a slowly wasting man.
> This is the sound of his death:
> but also of his living on.[16]

This is close in tone to the famous rhetoric of Pádraig Pearse and his vision of sacrifice, a belief that sustained the hunger strikers in the 1980s: the rhetoric that other Irish writers, such as O'Casey, have questioned and

---

13   Montague, *The Rough Field*, 35.
14   Montague, *The Rough Field*, 44–45.
15   Montague, *The Rough Field*, 46. Entitled 'Cage,' but subsequently reprinted in *Selected Poems* (London: Oxford University Press, 1982) and *New Selected Poems* (Meath: The Gallery Press, 1989) as 'The Cage.'
16   Montague, *Aquarius* (15/16, 1983/84), 80.

exposed. Indeed, discussing this very point in relation to Irish drama, Philip Edwards commented upon 'the intoxicating power of the language of romantic nationalism, a *damnosa hereditas*, which cannot be shaken off. If modern Irish drama is a drama of victims, they are chiefly victims of language.'[17] In this way, too, Montague makes poetry from the assimilation of the 'victim' with language and his own re-created sense of his 'self' as constituted by these same forces. As Nadine Gordimer has remarked in another context: 'There is no moral authority like that of sacrifice.'[18] This has obviously influenced the critical and historical terms of reference (and expectation) by which much, if not all, of Irish poetry has been received by readers and critics alike, particularly in the United States but also in Britain and Ireland. The important point to stress is that Montague's role in establishing these terms, both imaginatively and critically, anticipates the poetic negotiations a writer such as Seamus Heaney was to make in *Wintering Out* (1973) and *North* (1975).[19]

In his early experiences as an 'exile' of sorts, who returns on a voyage of rediscovery, his country origins framed by the colonizer's tongue, in a political state not of his or his family's making or choosing, Montague represents an identifiable pattern in his life and art. One consolidates the other in recognizable, even predictable, ways, so that the creative triangle (poetry as wound, victim of language, and the *inherited* sense of self seen as essential characteristics of Irish literature and history) forms an almost archetypal mandatory ritual, irresistible in its appeal to writer and audience alike:

> Grounded for the second time
> my tongue became a rusted hinge
> until the sweet oils of poetry

---

17   Philip Edwards, *Threshold of a Nation: A Study in English and Irish Drama* (Cambridge: Cambridge University Press, 1979), 232.

18   Nadine Gordimer, *The Essential Gesture: Writing, Politics and Places* (London: Jonathan Cape, 1988), 294.

19   Montague says as much himself in 'Dennis O'Driscoll: An Interview with John Montague,' *Irish University Review*, 19, 1 (Spring, 1989), 60: '… I ante-date this new emphasis on Ulster writing. I mean I had done *Poisoned Lands, Death of a Chieftain* and I was working on *The Rough Field*. I have described myself as the missing link of Ulster poetry.'

eased it and light flooded in.[20]

In the background of Montague's poetry there is that much-quoted passage from Joyce's *A Portrait of the Artist as a Young Man* when, facing the Dean of Studies, Stephen thinks:

> The language in which we are speaking is his before it is mine. How different are the words *home, Christ, ale, master,* on his lips and on mine! I cannot speak or write these words without unrest of spirit. His language, so familiar and so foreign, will always be for me an acquired speech. I have not made or accepted its words. My voice holds them at bay. My soul frets in the shadow of his language.[21]

Joyce's fictional character and Joyce's own obsessive and unique relationship with the English language aesthetically sustains Montague. One need only turn to Seamus Heaney's *Station Island* (1984) for further illustration of this resilient theme of Joycean estrangement in language, 'so familiar and so foreign'. So dominant is it in effect that, unlike the 'Big House/Ascendancy' motif in Irish writing, little discussion has taken place as to how relevant Stephen Dedalus's words actually are *now* to Irish experience and the social and political realities of the island, notwithstanding the powerful universal appeal of Joyce's story.

III

In John Bayley's *The Uses of Division*, the chapter that deals with the poetry of John Berryman, Robert Lowell, and Philip Larkin contains the following remark:

> The public status and recognition of poets in Russia, in the smaller European countries or in Spanish America, puts them in a different class: to be a national poetic rhetorician, like Mayakovsky or Neruda, is to be in some sense naive, to achieve

---

20   John Montague, 'A Flowering Absence,' *The Dead Kingdom*, 91.
21   James Joyce, *A Portrait of the Artist as a Young* Man (London: Jonathan Cape, 1920), 215.

power through naiveté. And not to be *taken in*, not to be thus socially and nationally innocent, is vital to the working of the poetry we are discussing.²²

The section of the chapter from which this quotation comes is called 'The Self as Available Reality' (after R. P. Blackmur) and it represents the kind of tension that characterizes the poetry of John Montague. For his work is caught between two poles of attraction: the 'national poetic rhetoric' and 'naïveté' of an acquired outrage and bitterness, as exhibited in *The Rough Field*, ranged against the later Lowellesque self-dramatizations of *The Dead Kingdom*. As Bayley remarks in the second section, 'The Importance of Elsewhere': 'It is difficult not to conclude that the dynamic of today's [1976] best poetry is a setting up in it of the poet, which, when accomplished, constitutes an aesthetic goal. The poet has arrived in our midst, his newness defined by the personal reality of the self his art has brought to us.'²³

In Montague the aesthetic goal is the personal reality, making an imaginative home for himself out of a powerful, monolithic, and conservative literary and cultural tradition. This means that, like a divining rod, his imagination wavers from the assembled sequences of love lyrics and recollection in *The Great Cloak* and *The Dead Kingdom* to the epical aspiration of attempting a poetry that will be shaped through (and in turn shape?) an entire community's history, torn by moral, political, and cultural division, such as he finds in the north of Ireland:

> Lines of leaving
> > lines of returning
> the long estuary
> > of Lough Foyle, a
> ship motionless
> > in wet darkness
> mournfully hooting
> > as a tender creeps
> to carry passengers

---

22   John Bayley, *The Uses of Division: Unity and Disharmony in Literature* (London: Chatto & Windus, 1976), 165.
23   Bayley, *The Uses of Division: Unity and Disharmony in Literature*, 177.

>   back to Ireland
> a child of four
>   this sad sea city
> my landing place[24]

Personal reality here assumes historical proportions. The poet inherits the past a priori and the poetry conveys, again compliantly, an already given self-identity: 'a child of four / this sad sea city / my landing place.'

Ironically, perhaps, when glossing this poem, Montague seemed to advocate 'a deliberate programme of denationalization', but went on to say that 'all true experiments and exchanges only serve to illuminate the self, a rediscovery of the oldest laws of the psyche'.[25] Yet it is true to say that much of Montague's own poetry is bound up with the nation-place and nationalism, with what he has called 'our racial drama of conscience'.[26] Irish mythology, in the form of Lir's daughters, is never far from the surface and many of his poems deal with Irish cultural icons; for example, the Irish landscape or the 'loss' of the Irish language. Furthermore, an elegy like 'Ó Riada's Farewell' – 'pride of music / pride of race' – concerning the premature death of the musician and composer Seán Ó Riada, carries a talismanic significance in recent Irish poetry.[27] It is in this poem that one sees clearly enough Montague's intention of restoring to life what he had earlier called, in 'The Road's End', the 'shards / of a lost culture'[28] since 'Ó Riada's Farewell' hears Ezra Pound's flourish, 'To have gathered from the air a live tradition'.[29] The poem provides a useful text in more ways than one since it

---

24 Montague, *The Rough Field*, 73.
25 John Montague, 'The Impact of International Modern Poetry on Irish Writing,' *The Figure in the Cave and other Essays*, 219.
26 Montague, 'The Impact of International Modern Poetry on Irish Writing,' *The Figure in the Cave*, 213.
27 Cf. Thomas Kinsella, 'A Selected Life & Vertical Man,' *Fifteen Dead* (Dublin: Dolmen Press, 1979); Seamus Heaney, 'In Memoriam Seán Ó Riada,' *Field Work* (London: Faber and Faber, 1979), and Seán Lucy, '*Unfinished Sequence* for Seán Ó Riada,' *Unfinished Sequence* (Dublin: Wolfhound Press, 1979).
28 Montague, *A Chosen Light* (London: MacGibbon and Kee, 1967), 32.
29 Montague, *A Slow Dance*, 57.

shows how, in the characteristic gesture of lament, memorializing the past and life of one person goes beyond the celebration of the solely human:

> And a nation mourns:
> The blind horseman with his harp carrying servant,
> Hurrying through darkness to a great house
> Where a lordly welcome waits, as here [.].[30]

What is more, the poem itself is an act of redeeming what has gone or lost: for 'defeat' read 'aisling': 'After another defeat, to be redeemed/ By the curlew sorrow of an asiling.' The imagination, lodged in the heroic past, converts its failures (Kinsale, Limerick, Aughrim) to compensatory images of acceptance, the 'curlew sorrow' of the impoverished present. However, this process, of 'a lost pastoral rhythm', asks a central question of Montague's own imaginative priorities and the extent to which he has created, in John Bayley's words, 'supreme beauty out of ugliness, emptiness and contingency, the trapped and the doomed … (while keeping) us continuously interested in himself, always wanting to hear more about him'. This is the real *aesthetic* risk a prolific autobiographical poet such as John Montague takes, given the cultural agenda he has set for himself:

> Dia dhuit
> *Dia agus Muire dhuit*
>   *Dia agus Muire*
> *agus Padraig dhuit*
>   invocation of powers
> to cleanse the mind.
>   Then the question
> and answer.
>   'What did she say?'[31]

---

30   Montague, *A Slow Dance*, 62.
31   Montague, *A Chosen Light*, 37.

IV

It is the 'thousand years' that stands as a metaphorical locus to most of John Montague's poetry; the ancestral haunting of the present as much as the present obscuring the past.[32] Montague attempts to embody this duality, and the most revealing aspect of his work is its sense of foreboding, an anticipation of closure and completion. For his poems deal in half-light, dawns or dusks, elusive moments of recollection, when the frisson of political or sexual tension has passed and the poet draws attention to their significance. This narrative urge to resolve his poems can falter, however, and lead into the clichéd rhetoric of, for instance, his poem in memory of Hugh MacDiarmid, 'Scotia', from *Mount Eagle*: 'Nourishing a lonely dream of how/this desolate country might have been!'[33] Whereas in 'Discords', also from *Mount Eagle*, the rhetorical question that closes the first section of the poem carries a personally charged vindication clearly absent from the ceremonial poems such as 'Scotia': 'For if they did not love each other/ Why should they heed a single word?'[34]

These two persistent directions of Montague's writing – one autobiographical, the other explicitly cultural – can find themselves insufficiently sustained by a distinct imaginative raison d'être. This lack means that some of Montague's poetry has a conventional air of being written to a prefabricated formula, with certain stock images and characters guaranteeing the 'Irish' authenticity of his work.[35] This may be linked to an awareness of what Stephen Spender outlined in the introduction to his study of Anglo-American sensibilities, *Love-Hate Relations*. When describing the contrasting attractions of the American writer for Europe (and England) as

---

32 Thus the three-faced stone-head (c.3rd–2nd B.C.) that adorns the cover of *New Selected Poems* (1989).
33 Montague, *Mount Eagle*, 61.
34 Montague, *Mount Eagle*, 45.
35 Cf. Richard J. Loftus, *Nationalism in Modern Anglo-Irish Poetry* (Madison and Milwaukee: University of Wisconsin Press, 1964), 16–17. This study remains one of the best readings of modern Irish poetry.

against the establishing of a 'native' literature (Williams v. Eliot), Spender comments on the 'connection between their separate existence [autobiography] and their country, in its history, landscape and people'. He goes on:

> This awareness is of a life which is that of an ideal United States or England which the writer, if he is in a correct relation to it, relates in his work. Unless he does have such a relation, his work will be peripheral to the centre or turned inward on himself. It follows that if the nation itself presents conditions which prevent the writer identifying it with the ideal of the country of the mind, then he will find himself opposed to the official nation. His work will find its centre in a patriotism against which he measures the surrounding public nation. To simplify my argument let me call the idea of a true nation, 'the patria'.[36]

In Ireland, the modern 'idea of a true nation' has of course been efficiently repossessed and institutionalized by the political course of nationalism and poets were (*are*?) generally seen as guardians of that sacred, rather than civic, duty.[37] There are many questions at issue here. One thinks, for example, of the complicated relationship between 'old' and 'new' cultures and of how, paradoxically, a *nation* like Ireland is both, simultaneously. There is also the sense in which 'the patria' in Spender's terms can be viewed autobiographically as the individual's generalized search for a father figure; the nation, his or her home; the idealized community, the family. Or, more specifically, the manner in which a poet like Montague sees himself consciously as a bridge between these divides of American, European, and Irish cultures in his own life and through his own writing. Thus, as he states in 'The Impact of International Modern Poetry on Irish Writing' (1973), one senses the ground being cleared for his own role: 'The only literary art in which we have not made our presence felt is the one in which we are supposed to excel: this is, poetry. Yeats apart,

---

36   Stephen Spender, *Love-Hate Relations: A Study of Anglo-American Sensibilities* (London: Hamish Hamilton, 1974), p. xiii. It is remarkable that no equivalent study has to date been undertaken in Anglo-Irish or Anglo-American literary and cultural sensibilities.

37   In Seamus Heaney's terms: 'The landscape was sacramental, instinct with signs, implying a system of reality beyond the visible realities.' 'The Sense of Place' (1974) in *Preoccupations: Selected Prose 1968–1978* (London: Faber and Faber, 1980), 132.

few Irish poets have been accepted as international figures in the way that Pablo Neruda is, or Octavio Paz, or Ungaretti.'[38]

The essential point I take from Spender's introduction concerns 'patria', the national ground out of which 'international figures' emerge, set alongside the 'ideal United States or England [or Ireland] which the writer, if he is in correct relation to it, releases in his work'. Whatever qualifications one may have about that phrase 'correct relation', the ideal Ireland that has been released in John Montague's poetry is effectively *now* the official version. One can go a step further and suggest that a possible reading of Montague's poetry is that, from a northern republican perspective, it concludes the cultural (and I stress *cultural*) agenda of twentieth-century Irish literary nationalism. Furthermore, Montague has insisted upon the non-English, 'European' dimension of Irish literature. His comments on exile in 'The Impact of International Modern Poetry on Irish Writing' are a case in point, as are his remarks on Louis MacNeice, whose work Montague sees 'very much in the non-experimental tradition of English modern poetry, and, as such, nearly unexportable'.[39]

Matters of trade apart, somewhat later in the same broadcast, when describing the poetry of Denis Devlin and Austin Clarke in terms of 'our racial drama of conscience', Montague proclaims that while 'difficult to define (perhaps because the imperial habit dies hard, and the British Council is a more subtle version of the *Pax Britannica*) an Irish writer has a better chance of being a European than has an Englishman'.[40] Yet such potential is qualified in Montague's mind by the injunction that 'if one is going to be influenced by contemporary poetry outside Ireland, it should be at first hand and not by hearsay, years after the event'.[41]

---

38 Montague, *The Figure in the Cave*, p. 210. 'The Impact of International Modern Poetry on Irish Writing' was originally broadcast on Radio Telefís Eireann as part of a series of talks, *Irish Poets in English*, and subsequently was published under that title in a collection edited by Seán Lucy (Cork: The Mercier Press, 1973).
39 Montague, *The Figure in the Cave*, 211.
40 Montague, *The Figure in the Cave*, 213.
41 Montague, *The Figure in the Cave*, 216.

The imperative sense here of the contemporaneity of poetry and the necessarily *positive* value of 'influences' per se are recalled in Montague's follow-on comment to the effect that having 'participated in one of the early readings of *Howl*, I found it depressing when the Ginsberg wave broke over Ireland a decade later, drowning many potential young poets'.[42]

The subjective reading assumes an impersonal critical status, yet who these 'young poets' were is left out of the account. They represent an audience of failure somewhat remote ('hearsay') from where the poet himself is – at the heart of things: 'We move in a world which is increasingly both local *and* international, and in poetry, as in science, there is nothing so irrelevant as repeating someone else's experiments.'[43]

Montague includes in his talk an admonition of the 'majority of Irish poets' who write 'as though Pound, Lawrence, Williams, had not brought a new music into English poetry, as though the iambic line still registered the curve of modern speech'.[44] Against this 'majority' failure on most sides, Montague requests, in a characteristic flourish, that 'like a composer or a painter, an Irish poet should be familiar with the finest work of his contemporaries, not just the increasingly narrow English version of modern poetry, or the more extensive American one, but in other languages as well'. He goes on:

> I would say that my contemporaries are not just the Irish poets I admire, but those with whom I feel an affinity elsewhere, Ponge in France, Octavio Paz in Mexico, Gary Snyder and Robert Duncan in San Francisco. I seem to be advocating a deliberate programme of de-nationalization, but all true experiment and exchanges only serve to illuminate the self, a rediscovery of the oldest laws of the psyche.[45]

So we are back at that intersection of 'a thousand years', with the added presence of nominated international figures at the crossroads. It is important to remind ourselves of the date for this broadcast – 1973 – and of how it was in the late 1960s and early 1970s that other voices, indisputably Irish in experience and accent, confidently familiar with developments in

---

42 Montague, *The Figure in the Cave*, 216.
43 Montague, *The Figure in the Cave*, 216.
44 Montague, *The Figure in the Cave*, 218.
45 Montague, *The Figure in the Cave*, 219.

European and American poetry and trained in English literature, were establishing themselves in the forefront of the public mind and critical press: poets such as Seamus Heaney, Derek Mahon, Eavan Boland, Seamus Deane, and Michael Longley. Freed from any need to prove themselves or the ground of their being poets (northern or otherwise), they moved with self-determination, absorbing in the main the artistic legacy of W. B. Yeats, rather than the leftovers of his cultural program, such as it was.

'Denationalization' as applied to the poetry of any one of these poets sounds incongruous, out of place, and as dated as Montague's exhortation that his fellow Irish poets must look beyond their own immediate borders. Such transcendence is imaginatively assumed in the work of these other poets and is also one of the central intellectual preoccupations in the critical writings of Heaney and Deane.[46]

In this sense John Montague has been vindicated by the example of his younger peers whose very difference challenges any deterministic or inherited formulation of what a poet should or should not do, read, or write about. The only exigencies are the recognition of individual talent and the limits of tradition.

There is the unimpeachable wisdom of Philip Larkin's comment to bear in mind in this regard. When responding to a request from D. J. Enright for a brief statement of his views on poetry, Larkin replied:

> I find it hard to give any abstract views on poetry and its present condition as I find theorising on the subject no help to me as a writer. In fact it would be true to say that I make a point of not knowing what poetry is or how to read a page or about the function of myth. It is fatal to decide, intellectually, what good poetry is because you are then in honour bound to try to write it, instead of the poems that only you can write.[47]

---

46   Cf. Seamus Heaney, *The Government of the Tongue* (London: Faber and Faber, 1988) and Seamus Deane, *Celtic Revivals* (London: Faber and Faber, 1985).

47   Philip Larkin, *Required Writing: Miscellaneous Pieces 1955–1982* (London: Faber and Faber, 1983), 79. It is interesting to compare Larkin's remark with Seamus Heaney's similar comment in 'Feeling into Words' (1974): '... it is dangerous for a writer to become too self-conscious about his own processes: to name them too definitively may have the effect of confining them to what is named.' *Preoccupations*, 52.

It is an early example, from 1955, of Larkin-speak, deceitfully sharp-witted *and* intuitive, preserving the private, secretive sources of his own imagination, and bluntly refusing to budge or reveal anything of himself. With certain changes in register, this could be Cavafy speaking, but the stabilizing force and composure of the English tradition in poetry acts like a rudder behind the concluding phrase, 'the poems that only you can write'. For the sense of who 'you' are as a writer strikes me as being one of, if not *the*, most important themes in John Montague's writing. His poetry and criticism (and fiction, for that matter) believe in the rhetorical weight of showing what *should* be done, read, claimed, written about, in order that a local field, like Garvaghey, can enjoy as much imaginative light as will also illuminate the amenable profiles of one's self. This is the insistently moral ambience of Montague's work, which sees the autobiographical and cultural as one and the same recurrent imaginative project: the poet as oracle; invoker of powers. In this regard Montague is very much more a traditionalist than he would have us believe from his comments on experimentalism, international writing, and so on. His poetry is lodged firmly in the custodianship of generous images of the good,[48] rather than in the quicksand of a modernism either fiercely introverted or aggressively peripheral.[49]

In establishing, or re-establishing this ancient territorial rite, Montague probably made it possible for a poet like Seamus Heaney to speak out of his own experience without loss of face, or for that matter, of faith in the mythic possibilities of poetry.

Yet throughout Montague's poetry there is a stylization of experience that is essentially literary, and that works against its epic grain. It is as if the poet were self-consciously setting out to prove something – about his past and its potency as a poetic theme. This side to Montague's poetry is characteristic of quite a lot of Irish writing in the 1970s and 1980s. As critics rarely fail to remind us, it has a direct bearing upon the colonized basis of English as a language spoken and written in Ireland. Certainly,

---

48   From Montague's poem, 'Waiting': 'some / Generous natural image of the good' in *The Great Cloak*, 56.
49   To pick up again on Spender's terms of reference in *Love-Hate Relations*, xiii.

the bardic strain associated with the tradition of Irish poetry in Gaelic breaks through Montague's poems and reveal a world strangely subsumed in the highly polished and achieved form of its expression, as in some of Montague's best-known lyrics – 'The Wild Dog Rose', 'The Sean Bhean Bocht', and 'A Lost Tradition'.

John Montague stands as the epitome of that dominant view of Irish poetry that derives from the national ideas, heritage, and messianic ideals forged as the cultural foundation of the Irish state and rehearsed in the mind and experience of one of its prodigal sons.[50] He sees his work as an artist strictly and reverentially as the sexual, political, and cultural communion of his life with its natural homeland, in the creation of an internationally recognizable identity, the 'Irish Poet'.

[1992]

---

50 See Loftus, *Nationalism in Modern Anglo-Irish Poetry*; in particular chapters 1, 2, 3, and 6.

CHAPTER 7

Potent Music: Yeats's Legacy

In January 1939, W. B. Yeats died and was buried in France. After the hostilities of the Second World War had ceased, he was finally laid to rest in 1948 in a Church of Ireland graveyard at Drumcliff, County Sligo. His work as a poet was traded for his name and we were bequeathed a phenomenon: *Yeatsian*.

Two things happened in the decades that separate us from Yeats's death. For many in Ireland and elsewhere, knowledge of his poetry depended largely upon a few hardy annuals that recurred in anthologies kept at home or the teaching texts at school: 'The Fiddler of Dooney', 'The Lake Isle of Innisfree', and some of the more 'difficult' poems such as 'Leda and the Swan' and 'Byzantium'. Simultaneously, Yeats became an industry, with an entire academic mill churning out critical volumes on his life, poetry, drama, prose writing, reading, and mythologies. Between the two worlds – of either scant familiarity or the monumental expert consumption of Yeats and what he stood for as an individual public figure – we lost sight of Yeats the poet.

Critics and scholars will argue until the cows come home about who and what the essential Yeats is precisely. Many see him as an old right-wing fogey who is tainted for life by his brief flirtation with Irish national socialism; others mock him as a relic of Auld Dacency, his head in the clouds, best left to tourist promoters of an Ireland no longer (if ever) real. But can there actually be a central core to any writer's work, we might like to ask? After all, times change and our ways of seeing things alter and in so doing radically affect what we look at, as much as how we do the looking.

One fact is indisputable: the international standing of Irish poetry is due to William Butler Yeats. His achievement, principally as a poet but also as a critic, dramatist, and polemicist for Irish cultural nationalism, is the pivotal point around which the direction of Irish poetry is most often drawn. There is a contradiction here. For, in spite of the tremendous influence Yeats exerted throughout his own lifetime – in Ireland and Europe, the United States and across language barriers worldwide – his poetic legacy within Ireland has taken a back seat to the cultural and poetical significance of his life and times. This is the context in which critics have debated his poetry. The artistic inheritance, by comparison, remains somewhat unacknowledged.

During his long life, however, W. B. Yeats transformed Irish poetry (in the English language) from its uncertain beginnings in the nineteenth century – the sprawling mythological epics of Sir Samuel Ferguson, the martial ballads of Thomas Davis, James Clarence Mangan's exotic and introverted autobiographical masques – into a language of what he was to call 'passionate syntax'. In 'To Ireland in the Coming Times' (*The Rose*, 1893), Yeats proclaims his allegiance to the company of Davis, Mangan, and Ferguson as poets who

> … sang to sweeten Ireland's wrong,
> Ballad and story, rann and song;
> Nor be I any less of them,
> Because of the red-rose-bordered hem
> Of her, whose history began
> Before God made the angelic clan,
> Trails all about the written page.[1]

During the turbulent years ahead, Yeats continuously redefined this allegiance, as Ireland lurched first into class struggle (the 1913 Lockout), rebellion and executions (Easter 1916), then into the War of Independence (1919–1921) before the state was actually founded, albeit within a partitioned country.

'September 1913', for instance, opens with a powerful sense of disillusionment that the high lofty ideals of nationalists such as Yeats's friend and mentor, John O'Leary, had ignominiously dwindled into conniving religiosity and commercial self-interest:

---

1 W. B. Yeats, 'To Ireland in the Coming Times,' *Yeats's Poems*, ed. A. Norman Jeffares (Basingstoke: Palgrave, 1996), 85.

> What need you, being come to sense,
> But fumble in a greasy till
> And add the halfpence to the pence
> And prayer to shivering prayer, until
> You have dried the marrow from the bone?[2]

Most critics agree that *Responsibilities* (1914), the collection from which this poem comes, marks a substantial change in Yeats's poetry, with diction and rhythm much more clearly defined. Probably under the influence of his friend Ezra Pound, who was acting as a secretary to him at this time (1913–1914), Yeats broke from the customary crepuscular ambiguities that had characterized the earlier poetry, and created in collections such as *Responsibilities* and *The Wild Swans at Coole* (1919), a stark imagistic simplicity unburdened with literary conceit:

> The trees are in their autumn beauty,
> The woodland paths are dry,
> Under the October twilight the water
> Mirrors a still sky [.][3]

The remaining twenty years of his life were to prove remarkably creative for Yeats the poet. He pursued his own intuitive needs into the supernatural, an obsession since he was a young man, and simultaneously proposed a view of civilization and history that, while veering towards the fascist movements current in the late twenties and thirties, insisted upon the essential integrity and significance of the poetic imagination to the modern world.

In poems such as 'The Fisherman' and 'Ego Dominus Tuus' (*The Wild Swans at Coole*) Yeats explored his ambition, as in the former poem, to write 'one / Poem maybe as cold / And passionate as the dawn', conscious, all the while, as he stated in 'Ego Dominus Tuus', that

> ... art
> Is but a vision of reality.

2   W. B. Yeats, 'To Ireland in the Coming Times,' *Yeats's Poems*, ed. A. Norman Jeffares 'September 1913', 210.
3   W. B. Yeats, 'The Wild Swans at Coole,' 233.

> What portion in the world can the artist have
> Who has awakened from the common dream
> But dissipation and despair?[4]

It is the rhetorical question that Yeats's poetry constantly sought to answer, sometimes in an over-elaborate symbolic construction, like 'The Phases of the Moon', but also in the naturalistic style and poignancy of 'Easter 1916' or 'Sixteen Dead Men', where contemporary life is turned into art.

Never far from Yeats's mind, though, was his particular sense of himself as a poet and the need to create a suitable landscape and a vision of life that could house his imagination. In 'Sailing to Byzantium' Yeats wishes to dwell, figuratively, in 'the artifice of eternity', celebrating, with an almost Keatsian sensuousness, the glorious Byzantine world, 'to sing … / Of what is past, or passing, or to come'.[5] This desire always gives way in Yeats's poetry to a rigorous refusal to give up on the world. While there are many poems in which he curses modernity and what he sees as its graceless and glum unheroic failings, Yeats returns to that 'real' world, often with a vengeance, as in 'Blood and the Moon':

> There, on blood-saturated ground, have stood
> Soldier, assassin, executioner,
> Whether for daily pittance or in blind fear,
> Or out of abstract hatred, and shed blood …[6]

In sequences such as 'The Tower', 'Meditations in Time of Civil War', 'Nineteen Hundred and Nineteen' – all published in *The Tower* – and 'Blood and the Moon', Yeats set down powerfully forthright terms of reference for those poets who were publishing or beginning their writing careers in the mid-to-late thirties. This ensured that in his *Last Poems* (1936–1939), Yeats spoke with an indisputable authority, not only on the recent history of his country, a history that he and friends like Lady Gregory had in part shaped, but also, more crucially, of the place that he had confirmed

---

4   W. B. Yeats, 'Ego Dominus Tuus,' 265.
5   W. B. Yeats, 'Sailing to Byzantium,' 301.
6   W. B. Yeats, 'Blood and the Moon,' 351.

for poetry in Irish life, and vice versa. When Yeats summoned the literary and political figures (John O'Leary, Standish O'Grady, Maud Gonne) associated with his past as 'All the Olympians; a thing never known again', the implicit judgement on the world he was soon to leave was clear. It did not measure up to his expectations and consequently, as he wrote in 'The Statues':

> We Irish, born into that ancient sect
> But thrown upon this filthy modern tide
> And by its formless spawning fury wrecked,
> Climb to our proper dark, that we may trace
> The lineaments of a plummet-measured face.[7]

Yeats's aim during his life (and, in terms of legacy, for some time thereafter), was to elevate 'We Irish' to an appropriate place ('our proper dark') in the world that would, by example, reject the modern tide's 'formless spawning'. The impressive scope, idealistic ambition, and imaginative demands of such a vision encouraged other poets, such as F. R. Higgins, unwisely to emulate it, with little artistic success. Higgins's poet-friend Austin Clarke also started by imitating Yeats's epic range, then slowly and steadily realized after a period of artistic silence, bracketed by *Night and Morning* (1938) and *Ancient Lights* (1955), that the poet must follow his own imaginative light and not bask in one as powerful as Yeats's.

Patrick Kavanagh, even at some remove, was greatly influenced by the cultural ideals and literary dominance of Yeats's writing. In some of his earlier work, one hears the strain of Irish pastoralism that Yeats had promoted, but Kavanagh grew to despise 'Irishness' and rejected out of hand what he saw as the suffocating provincialism of the Irish literary scene, still caught in the spider's web of Yeats's writing or looking over its collective shoulder for approval to London.

The intellectual orientation of poets Denis Devlin and Brian Coffey had little in common with the pre-eminence of Yeats or his immediate poetic descendants. While taking their roots from modernist poets Ezra Pound and T. S. Eliot, the artistic discipline of James Joyce, and drawing

---

7   W. B. Yeats, 'The Statues,' 460.

upon continental literary movements, such as surrealism, and on French poetry, they sought to create a literature that was, in its sophistication and allusive concentration, free from overtly regional or national bearings.

Indeed, it could be said that with the death of Yeats and throughout the immediate aftermath of the Second World War, Ireland was cut off from the necessary wider cosmopolitan audience upon which poets like Coffey and Devlin and their contemporaries such as Ethna MacCarthy, depended. Ireland's policy of neutrality, however, confounded the English-based northern Irish poet Louis MacNeice (who wrote a very fine book on Yeats in 1941) and drove a metaphorical wedge between the two parts of the country, reinforcing the seemingly different and contrasting paths Northern Ireland and the Republic of Ireland were to follow. This division strengthened the claims of poets such as John Hewitt in seeing the north of Ireland as a separate and distinctive region within the entire country, laying down the imaginative possibility in the 1940s and 1950s for a well-charted renaissance of poetry in the province later on. When this actually did come about in the 1960s and 1970s, the stimulus came not alone from MacNeice and Hewitt, but included the vigorous self-awareness and colloquial manner of Patrick Kavanagh, who was brought up near the border in County Monaghan, and John Montague's reimagining of Ulster in global terms.

Roughly during this same period of the 1950s and 1960s, the poetry of Thomas Kinsella was charting its own course, highly mannered, austere, and very conscious of the great changes in the writing of poetry that had taken place outside Ireland.

At the heart of what Richard Murphy writes, too, there is a troubled confrontation between past and present, but what marks out Murphy is the refined equipoise of his poetry, derived in part from his southern Anglo-Irish background and its inherited sense of being caught, or time-locked, between two worlds – at once grandly imperial but also marooned and decaying. This abiding tension, paralleling Yeats's, is finely contained by Murphy's formally distant, architectural designs, most noticeably in his collection *The Price of Stone* (1985).

The precise poetic legacy of Yeats is to be found, however, in the style and structure of Derek Mahon's poetry. For Mahon, Belfast born and from a Protestant background, has drawn imaginatively upon Yeats's 'big' stanzas, rigorously positioned syntax, and rhetorical eloquence, most noticeably in one of his best-known poems, 'A Disused Shed in Co. Wexford'. However, Yeats's cultural nationalism has been rewritten and radicalized in the writings of Seamus Deane, poet-critic and driving force behind much of the publishing activity of the 1980s and 1990s Derry-based theatre company Field Day, whose board included poets Seamus Heaney and Tom Paulin, both of whom have engaged Yeats on an artistic and polemical level.

Of course, Yeats's influence has continued to bridge national boundaries, as well as generations, since W. H. Auden wrote his famous elegy 'In Memory of W. B. Yeats' in 1939. American poets such as Theodore Roethke and John Berryman have noted the significance of Yeats in their own artistic lives while one of England's most popular post-war poets, Philip Larkin, tells the story of his three years 'trying to write like Yeats, not because I liked his personality or understood his ideas but out of infatuation with his music'.[8]

For quite different reasons too, what Larkin called Yeats's 'potent music' has also inspired African, Palestinian, and South American writers who sought to give, in Seamus Deane's words, 'a voice and a history to those who have been deprived of both'. We should never discount this revolutionary example of Yeats's life and writing.

From the heady early lyrics and perfect imitations of ballads, to the passionate speech and architectural splendour of the sequences, the obsessions and self-doubts of his later work, Yeats's self-consciousness as a poet was always creatively deployed in the interest of the poem. The artistic and the polemical crossed in Yeats's imagination.

His imagination rested upon what literally surrounded him – the Irish countryside, which he saw so completely: the rural towns like Gort, the isolated districts like Ballylee, and the glorious beauty spots such as Ben Bulben and Innisfree. He imagined forests, streams, lakes, mountains as all having their own spirit that poetry could in some way embody. He heard the accents and rhetoric of street talk, committee rooms, clubs, and the

---

8   Philip Larkin, 'Introduction to *The North Ship*,' in *Required Reading: Miscellaneous Pieces 1955–1982* (London: Faber and Faber, 1983), 29.

drawing rooms of the Big House, as well as the literary buzz of London and Paris, amongst other cities. He captured with individual flourish ideals – of individual, nature, and nationalism – that could be written out in verse. He could also see himself left alone without any illusions, 'caught in the cold snows of a dream.'[9]

Yeats wrote of sexuality and love; about possible esoteric ways of understanding the world and about the materialistic drives that can take over people's lives unless they are very careful. He was, let there be no mistake about it, very much his own man. The story of his life is told in his poems as autobiography literally becomes art. For Yeats, though, the emphasis was always on dynamic transformation, rather than passive self-confession. This poetry should resonate with us today, for, like him, we battle away trying to find some kind of balance between experience and innocence, those contrary states that one of Yeats's greatest poetic and spiritual mentors, William Blake, powerfully dramatized in lyrical and prophetic verse.

Turning from the twentieth to the twenty-first century, we can look back at Yeats making a similar journey from the nineteenth to the twentieth. Where he saw England's industrialized democracy despoiling the green and pleasant land of Ireland, we, who are 'Green', see this worldwide struggle to preserve the natural bounty and ecological grace of the earth, threatened by multinational conglomerates that tower over us and emasculated by theme parks and heritage centres. As Yeats heard and wrote out a new cultural notation for Irish self-perceptions, clouded and confused as they were by historical cross-signals, we too debate the meaning and viability of pluralism, gender equality, diversity, and national identity at a turbulent time of European federation. Where we look well beyond the institutions of religion for an understanding of life, he too experimented and explored other mystical sects like theosophy and spiritual practices from India. And in the conflicts of human friendship, companionship, love, and sexuality, Yeats was also there, sending back his report to whoever cared to listen.

Last, but by no means least, while we chivvy and demur about the role of the Artist, making too much or too little of what he or she can do, Yeats led by example – writing, campaigning, lecturing, touring, debating,

---

9   W. B. Yeats, 'Meditations in Time of Civil War: V The Road at My Door', X.

organizing, and tirelessly giving of his energies (to the point of exhaustion) in what he believed was the artist's responsibility to his audience. This could well be Yeats's greatest legacy, since he reminds us all now, writer and reader, performer and audience, that we are bound by the same rules of existence and when we set out to break them, we should know why. Yeats is the poet of limits par excellence, telling us who we are, where we come from, and what we should try to become – as individuals, as a nation and, indeed, as one earth.

[1993]

CHAPTER 8

Critical Mass

> Hostility to poetry, whether conscious or unconscious, begins when critics assume that poems and myths are only peculiar ways of making factual statements.[1]

I

The 1980s saw a major, if subtle, change happen in the social placing of writing in Ireland. Political patronage, commercial sponsorship, and public relations seemed to move hand in glove with the promotion of 'the Arts'. There was a steady ideological shift towards popularizing the arts in general. Editors, commentators, critics, and others in the media were encouraged to appear more popular and populist than the next, more tuned-in to the 'real' issues. As an indirect result, audiences became markets, symbols sales, prizes and awards promotion pitches, art 'an angle', and literary supplements, interviews, and profiles literally little more than gossip columns, seeking controversy, or recycled publishers' blurbs. Writing became fashionable, *very* fashionable.

Popularity, accessibility, and entertainment turned the key word of recognition into a byword for artistic success. What this all meant in creative and imaginative significance was no longer primary. Any hint of critical circumspection was caricatured as academic and elitist. And in a way this kind of aggressive eagerness *was* useful in so far as it blew away for good the cobwebs of the past that cloyingly gathered around the very (pious) idea of literature in Ireland. Similarly, the tired acquiescence in the impression

---

1   W. B. Stanford, *Enemies of Poetry* (London: Routledge & Kegan Paul, 1980), 3.

that writers were two-a-penny and taken very much for granted, also went, more or less. The 1980s, ironically, gave a sense of dignity back to writers if only because writing was seen as a money-spinner – a good PR ploy.

Books, paintings, films, music – all were praised or sifted through on the pretext and strength of what they disclosed about the hidden Ireland of sexual repression, political hypocrisy, and so on. These were the days of 'self-disclosure' on a national scale – a literary equivalent of *The Oprah Winfrey Show*. Indeed the American parallel is there for all to see, if we are to go by what Robert Hughes has said:

> In America there's this astonishing lock between therapeutic sanctimony and the profit motive. Art is their church. It was sold to the raw republic as improving experience, in terms of spiritual edification. Nothing whatever to do with sensuous enjoyment or sharpening the old eye. Passionate moralising about the arts began very early on. So if you question this or, worse, say that something is rubbish, it's not an aesthetic disagreement but a moral one.[2]

The state of Irish art has become similarly influenced by a confessional morality. The morality is, too, the very kitbag that we hear and read about daily in the media. Journalism and art consequently draw ever closer, to such an extent that it can be difficult to tell them apart. The documentary imperative became dominant as Ireland turned this way and that, obsessively trying to find a new vision of, and for, itself. This insularity created, by turn, a species of superficial cosmopolitanism and, in reaction, a retrenched nativism that has not caught hold so far.

The symbolic moment came (and *had to*, as many justly believed) with the election as president of Mary Robinson in 1990. In that isolated event, an imagined alternative took root that overcame the familiar realities of Irish political and cultural life. The possibility presented itself (and still does) that coherently structured imaginative campaigns can change people's lives. More modestly, that they can influence how we perceive ourselves – which almost amounts to the same thing. Yet such genuine cause for celebration

---

2   Robert Hughes, 'Who Will Garde the Avante Garde?' *The Irish Times,* Weekend Section, 23 May 1992, 5.

should not eclipse the real and intransigent economic, moral, and political problems that the country faces.

In these circumstances, there is a danger that 'the Arts' are used as a kind of smokescreen for the lack of political will to tackle and resolve these issues. 'The Arts' are set up as a high-profiled, yet impotent, moral 'opposition'. Writing and writers run the risk of being conned into a game of pass-the-buck – bearing or beating the humanistic heart as institutional power and authority look on, bemused. But this show will not change much, and change is what is at issue now. It is at the core of all the current agendas – change for the better, based upon a more honest understanding of past failures.

But in the 1980s, the republic of letters became a commercial enterprise, an adjunct of the tourist business. Writing was looked upon in a materially different way than in previous years. It was a change, not of accent or emphasis, but of direction, ideologically linked to the altered perceptions that conservation centres and heritage theme parks enact regarding our relationship with nature, landscape, and history. This substantial cultural change was facilitated with little or no questioning and is almost now complete.

For it was much easier to get a poem published in Ireland in the 1980s than it was to find a job. Indeed, there may be some kind of curious link between an economic recession and the number of people who started to write poems or short stories. For those who may well have been quite happy living their lives thinking of 'some day' becoming writers, many have actually made that commitment, possibly on the basis that there was little else to do. Ireland is, we are told, a *literary* culture, so why not; what is there to lose?

Consequently, poetry is everywhere. Books are published by the new time – first collections are launched, sold on the night, occasionally reviewed, stockpiled, and sometimes poets are interviewed, given prizes, but, more than likely, books are forgotten within the year. This speed of turnover has become mind boggling for a country the size of Ireland, with its concentration of media in Dublin (or Belfast) producing high-visibility screenings of one writer or another, usually in the form of light entertainment. As one normally unacerbic writer remarked in a fit of pique: 'You can't throw a stone over your shoulder without hitting a poet on the head.'

Looked at in the clear light of unexasperated and impartial day, writing poetry is an activity that has consoled and given enjoyment to many hundreds of thousands of people, and long may it do so. There is the risk, though, that much of this writing is promoted as self-expression similar to the American obsession with poetry as therapy, public and private. Letting it all hang out can lead straight to poetic sag.

The problem begins (and ends) when the reception writing receives sidesteps any reasonably detailed literary evaluation in favour of a media coverage that is uninterested in, and often actively hostile to, poetry as an art form. Maybe there is a constitutional antipathy between both forms of communication? Eugenio Montale predicted in 1952 that art was developing into two directions: 'a utilitarian art not unlike sport for the masses' opposed to 'true art as such, not so different from the art of the past and not easily reducible to cliché'.[3] However one is to view the situation, writing became an alternative lifestyle in the Ireland of the 1980s. As Robert Hughes remarked of the New York art world then: 'Never had there been so many artists, so much vying for attention, so many collectors, so many inflated claims and so little sense of measure.'[4]

Names are in print, photographs taken, discussion (of a sort) follows, and out of the anonymity of a personal life, something 'greater' beckons. What that something is, is an illusory sense of freedom, of being a writer. But why should this be so? Why should writing in Ireland carry this extraordinary responsibility to offer up opportunities that are not available in the wider society?

In John McGahern's short story 'High Ground', an exchange takes place between the alcoholic schoolteacher, Master Leddy, and some of his former pupils:

> Ye had the brains. There are people in this part of the country digging ditches who could have been engineers or doctors or judges or philosophers had they been given the opportunity. But the opportunity was lacking. That was all that was lacking.[5]

---

3   Eugenio Montale, *The Second Life of Art: Selected Essays* (New York: The Ecco Press, 1982), 28.
4   Robert Hughes, *Nothing If Not Critical* (London: Collins Harvill 1990), 6.
5   John McGahern, *High Ground* (London: Faber and Faber, 1985), 102.

The 'opportunity was lacking': so in a society with closed access to opportunities, the tendency to view writing as a privileged alternative is very strong. Given then the unemployment disaster that was the 1980s, small wonder 'the Arts' became a viable career possibility and, within that, poetry was seen as form of expression and consolation sustained and promoted in a kind of public relations exercise, written about in terms of a 'social diary'.

The problem is that poetry is not *only* these things, which is precisely where Robert Hughes's 'sense of measure' comes in. Yet this issue of judgement and discrimination sits very uncomfortably on our shoulders in Ireland. To criticize goes against the grain and is perceived, colloquially, as a negative thing.

Patrick Kavanagh knew the difference of course – that artistic mastery is never easy and usually elusive. Much of his critical writings (some of the best work we have on Irish poetry from the inside) deals with this issue:

> For a man in Ireland to have the label 'poet' attached to him is little short of a calamity.... He becomes a sort of exhibit, not a man in and of the world. If he happens to be a dilettante without a passionate faith, he will enjoy this position but if he is a genuine poet, it is an indignity and something much worse. Therefore I announce here and now that I am speaking as a journalist. I have resigned from being a poet and I hope my resignation will be accepted.[6]

What Kavanagh meant here by 'genuine' is the big question, but his ironic mocking resignation asks another question: What happens to poetry (never mind poets) when 'popularity' (as distinct from popular culture) becomes the socially and culturally acceptable norm and literary criterion? For popularity is a tricky business and to rely upon it as a key to artistic value is questionable. I am not for a moment suggesting that literature depends on the anonymous, unread genius sitting alone in his or her mother's house, remote bungalow, or council flat. Anything but. What I am trying to identify is the kind of cultural priorities that emerged in Ireland during the 1980s and have become dominant, *specifically* in relation to the critical reception of poetry, but by implication literature as a whole.

6 Patrick Kavanagh, 'A Goat Tethered Outside the Bailey,' *The Bell* (September 1953), 27.

It often looked as if poets were being turned into commercial representatives who had to sell their 'selves' as wares. The critical interventions were based increasingly around polemical agendas with little relation to artistic achievement. This literary politics is, of course, caught up with the imaginary sense of the power that writing has in Irish society. It also involves, prosaically, state and private patronage, access to the media, and the struggle to establish 'a reputation'.

Writing on these themes, the poet and critic Les Murray remarked in *The Peasant Mandarin*:

> We must break the grace-and-favour approach to patronage, just as surely as we must break the link, discerned by the public with ruinous effect, between art and privilege. We have reneged on the old problem of reconciling equality with excellence, and we must take it up again, or else face a new pattern of oppressions and class gulfs.[7]

Reconciling equality with excellence sounds an honourable objective for any poet and anything that gets in the way of achieving it should be brushed aside. For example, this very notion of 'popularity'. So perhaps the 1980s in Ireland conceal deep-seated problems as much as show the real gains, such as the emergence of several woman poets of impressive stature including Eavan Boland, Eiléan Ní Chuilleanáin, Medbh McGuckian, Nuala Ní Domhnaill, and Paula Meehan. This breakthrough is the single most significant feature of the last decade.

Alongside this artistic achievement, one should also place the phenomenal success of Brendan Kennelly and Paul Durcan in not only reaching, but also *creating* a new audience for their poetry. This engagement with an audience on emotional and social terms, earthed in common, if unstated, moral and cultural assumptions, has a lot to do with the Ireland that emerged in the 1980s and tells us about that society, in turn.

It was an Ireland pitched into self-searching, shrugging off the coil of the church, sceptical of its politicians, losing confidence in its democracy, and desperately in need of finding out the truth about itself.

---

7   Les Murray, *The Peasant Mandarin* (Queensland: University of Queensland Press, 1978), 16.

Poets like Kennelly and Durcan, along with Boland and others, provided an answer, or a sounding board. And in the soundings they gave, they presented a prolific and ready reckoning that involves both the dark and lighter sides of the Republic's moral nature. Their poems privatize and secularize the confessional demands of the public state of mind, interrogate the traditional, historical roles, and see what is going on behind the closed doors of this home, or that institution. It was a society discovering itself, very much in transition.

To invoke critical standards or make artistic judgements in such a context is problematical, to say the least. Any hint of an engaged, practical criticism – of doubting the consensus – suggests heretical elitist leanings and privilege in the face of populism's cultural revolt. This ascendancy means effectively the controlling middle class of modern Ireland, listening out for itself or entertaining manageable images of its own place and a desired history of feeling instead of ideas.

It is important, therefore, that we nail all this cant about accessibility and so forth on the door of the last decade since, more often than not, what was at stake was a masked form of self-promotion and careerism – Robert Hughes's 'astonishing lock' of sanctimony and the profit motive. It has precious little to do with art if one considers when the last book by an English, American, Scottish, Caribbean, or Australian poet was reviewed in an Irish newspaper. And how is it possible for a literary editor (albeit half in jest) of a national newspaper to remark, only half in jest, that his pages do not review poetry or cookery books? Pressure on space plays two ways.

Hand-in-hand with the high visibility of poets in the 1980s, there was also this curious *indifference* towards the *value* of what 'got' written – the poem on the page, in other words, with *its* language, structure, shape as well as the world *it* assumes to embody and the voice that *it* articulates. Paralleling this indifference, the 1980s also saw, as we all know now, the extraordinary decay in our public life, and the draining away, via emigration as much as anything else, of the energy and vitality so necessary for the maintenance of a critically alert civic society. Both features define the poetic contours of our cultural life and vice versa.

Speaking of precisely this present, there is something significant (and poignant) in the relative isolation of a figure such as Thomas Kinsella – an implied indictment that he, in uncompromising terms, laid down in an interview in *The Irish Times*:

> Suspicious of the 'trivialising' current trends of appeasing the popular taste with 'accessibility' [Kinsella] criticises the poet as entertainer. 'Poetry should be concerned with communication, not entertainment.... It's not one of the lucky times. There's a lot of bad poetry, bad poets, bad artists and bad readers'.[8]

There is indeed, but this is *also* a lucky time, because things *are* changing. Who and what mediates these changes is important, be that in artistic or cultural (or indeed, political) terms. We must not make the mistake of falling for the politically *correct* statement and acceptable sentiment – regarding the North, for instance, or relations with Britain; or what Robert Hughes rightly calls 'the cant of cultural empire and nostalgia for the lost imperial centre'. In the busy-ness of such puritanical agendas, loaded with the prescription of sectional quotas, the poem loses out. And it is this vulnerability that makes poetry so incisive, unpredictable, and subversive. As Kavanagh knew, poetry destabilizes every impatient effort to turn it into something else. Otherwise a self-deluding and self-promoting chauvinism of the kind that he fought so hard against will descend upon us again.

Poetry does not fit into neat categories of decades, any more than actual life. And this idea of Poetry with a capital P does not really stand up either. It is all at best useful shorthand for general discussion. For there are only ever books of poems making up a world or a voice or an attitude of mind – a critical presence. Writers and artists believe passionately in the value of what they do. It is *that* imaginative ambition that needs protection to flourish in a culture convinced of its own ability to make the necessary discriminations from the ground up. This confidence is aesthetic *and* civic. It is also powerful. It is an ability and practice centrally linked to the educational and political priorities of any country and the way access to these learning and democratic institutions is maintained. Yet the 1980s made many unhappy with the quality of our democracy and as an indirect result, too much was looked for in the literature – and too little.

---

8   Thomas Kinsella, 'Thomas Kinsella: A Poet between Two Traditions,' *The Irish Times,* 3 December 1990, 10.

As García Márquez has said, the most revolutionary thing a writer can do is to write well. Committing the poem to a page, making that right, as well as experiencing the decency of mature critical consideration and the non-deferential respect of working artists, is, in this context, a political act, as Kavanagh put it, of being 'in and of the world'. What I am saying here is little more than that Ireland is now in the same situation as other English-speaking cultures in which the values of entertainment and advertising media have taken over (or overtaken) the complex values of art. Maybe there are no longer publicly acceptable *artistic* values, anyway, and the marketing men and women who sell 'units' once called 'books' have won out. In which case, there *can be* no distinction between the poem (play, film, sculpture, dance, song) and an advertisement, between the genuine and the dilettante. That this postmodern heaven has arrived on the wings of postindustrial capitalism is truly, efficiently apocalyptic.

[1993]

CHAPTER 9

The Parochial Idyll: W. R. Rodgers

I

There is a book to be written about the way Protestants from the north of Ireland imagine the rest of the country they live in. By which I mean 'Ireland': a fictional world rather than the actual place. For various reasons, this Ireland – as against the social, moral, and political world of the Republic and/or republicanism – is an alluring ideal. It has a fantasy life of its own. Musical, dreamy (alas), old-world-like; a kind of innocent state the Protestants themselves once belonged to or imagined themselves being cast out from, under pressure of the ineluctable demands of the modern, industrialized world. This attraction, which is a mix of the patronizing, the genuine, and the kitsch and naïve, may well prove, in the years ahead, an ironic lifesaver for the Irish language, and it could well be the source Protestants draw upon to find a new identity for themselves.

The intriguing thing about all this is that the fascination for things Irish, bordering on the voyeuristic, has been largely unexamined insofar as it relates to those writers in Ireland whose background is the Protestant north (shorthand, I know). We have read and heard a lot about differing relationships to landscape, but rarely, to my knowledge, have the sources and imaginative assumptions of writers like MacNeice, Rodgers, Hewitt, or, for that matter, F. R. Higgins, been scrutinized. For they wrote out of an artistic and intellectual preoccupation shadowed by this idealized picture of Ireland, or a reaction against it. Even MacNeice, who had a fairly sharp-witted purchase on what was going on around him, failed to understand the Republic (in the making and afterwards) while remarking, in his unfinished autobiography, *The Strings Are False*, on his sense of freedom at being in Dublin and his love affair with the west coast. Why there should be this double vision is not an intellectual question alone. It is at the heart of Irish twentieth-century Romanticism; for Yeats's 'We were the last romantics' left a powerfully pervasive legacy few escaped, particularly those poets who were overly sensitive about their own cultural identity.

Here was a state, established under the influence of artists such as Yeats, brought into being by other writers who had fought for it, like O'Faoláin and Peadar O'Donnell, and, in the Second World War, by default, perceived as a belligerent neighbour. The tone shifts when irritation creeps into *The Strings Are False* as the news of war breaking out reaches MacNeice in Galway. Forays are maintained from London after the war, as if returning to Ireland was re-entering the Old World – via rugby matches or the BBC radio programs Rodgers made on Irish writers. *The Character of Ireland*, a book on Ireland is planned but which MacNeice and Rodgers do not complete (Davin traces the background to this in his 'memoir' in the *Collected Poems of W. R. Rodgers*).

I will follow briefly this memoir's representative value as regards Rodgers poetry. It is about the greening of Rodgers. Dan Davin describes how Rodgers had been 're-created by Dublin' but the exchanges between Davin and the commissioned writers cast some light on my opening remarks. This is Rodgers to Davin:

> In a moment of insight (or drink) I suggested that Louis and I should devote the middle and hinging pages of the book to a pastoral hammer-and-tongs give-and take on Partition in which we might, as uncouth shepherds, say all the outrageous things which nobody dare put in urbane prose. Ireland forgives anything in poetry. Louis, I'm glad, likes the idea.[1]

As the two traipse around Ireland, it becomes obvious that no *The Character of Ireland* will appear other than as anecdotes of their travels, drinking, and further requests, once back in England, for expenses to visit Ireland again. In the late 1950s, Davin writes:

> If I would co-operate, with money, and let [Rodgers] have a session with Peadar O'Donnell. 'I'd get you the best stuff that ever was got under the Irish lamps'.[2]

---

[1] Dan Davin, 'A Memoir,' *Collected Poems of W. R. Rodgers*, (London: Oxford University Press, 1971), xiv.

[2] Davin, 'A Memoir,' *Collected Poems of W. R. Rodgers*, xvi.

This is Ireland as anthropological curio, a heart's desire and a great gas. It is the Ireland Rodgers tried to imagine in his poems too, under the contrary influence of MacNeice no doubt, but also of Dylan Thomas – not the wisest of artistic influences to follow. In the background, too, were the stricter and longer-lasting examples of 'the earlier English poets such as Herrick' who, according to Davin, Rodgers used in an effort to 'sidestep the rancorous antinomies of Ulster, and perhaps . . . re-create a parochial idyll'.[3] This is precisely what Rodgers sought to do, only to realize that the impossibility of any such project as *The Character of Ireland* also affected his own poetry. In 1963, the year of MacNeice's sudden death, a decade and more since the idea is first promulgated, Rodgers writes: 'Working on it both excites and depresses me, and I realise that to write about it is like opening an old wound, which is Ireland.'[4]

The following year, on another trip to Dublin for BBC recordings, Rodgers's comments are particularly revealing:

> Probably my reason in going [to Dublin] was to vivify my anger and love for the place and to find out why it was always so destructive to the likes of Louis and me. I think that I have found out part of the reason.... It wasn't an easy visit ... every day for five weeks I'd turn myself into a successful extrovert. I think I managed to do it, more equably than usual. But in the small hours of each morning my introverted mind, outraged, had to go mad. Æ – Yeats – Dev – Cosgrave etc – all the old timers – and all the old words I'd heard about them, would go berserk, come alive, and rampage through my brain with a will of their own but I managed to keep a hold, and to return to civilization.[5]

The long, tortuous path of *not* writing *The Character of Ireland* lasted right up to his death in 1969, unfinished and unfinishable. There is though, the extraordinary admission contained in the privacy of this letter of his acting out a role in Dublin ('turn myself'), the verbal energy with which he cannot cope ('the words ... go berserk') and the attempt to maintain control before the 'return to civilization'.

3   Davin, 'A Memoir,' *Collected Poems of W. R. Rodgers*, x.
4   Davin, 'A Memoir,' *Collected Poems of W. R. Rodgers*, xviii.
5   Davin, 'A Memoir,' *Collected Poems of W. R. Rodgers*, xx.

This is a psychological state as much as an intellectual issue and it takes on imaginative implications as well because Rodgers's own poetry embodies the conflict between all three points of this ideological tension. Rodgers tried to bluster it out with a generalized poetic rhetoric, while simultaneously trying to create a kind of Edenic world wherein this conflict of interest would simply cease to exist.

In the second volume of his autobiography, *The Middle of My Journey* (1990), John Boyd recalls how W. R. Rodgers would 'mount a pulpit and deliver a short sermon to a congregation of one – myself'.

> I cannot recall anything of what he said but he looked impressive standing slightly sideways as his usually soft voice resonated in the empty church. He loved words, perhaps he loved them too well, he was by nature a taciturn and diffident man who, when he was sober, used words sparingly, but when drunk he would scatter them so extravagantly that his hearers could hardly believe their ears.[6]

There is about Rodgers the sense of melancholia, mixed with devilment and anxiety, that often characterizes writers from a northern Protestant background of his generation. It was as if, located in London, but on frequent returns to Belfast, a cultural performance took place. This mask looked in various directions all at once.

Whether in Dublin on BBC business, traveling through 'Ireland', in Belfast for a few days with old friends, before returning to London, or in London BBC haunts, there is something desperately self-conscious about their 'Irishness'. In lesser writers, this anxiety becomes professional, such as the embarrassing sight of northern Protestants faking 'Irish' accents and what they consider to be Irish mannerisms.

That Rodgers was 'a tortured and guilt-ridden man for most of his adult life' adds a truly tragic dimension to his artistic achievement.[7] It is with the defining northern context of this achievement that Michael Longley begins his level-headed introduction to Rodgers's *Poems*:

> Ulster is still likely to produce poets who write out of a response to religion. Like his friend Louis MacNeice, Rodgers was motivated by strong anti-puritan feelings.

6   John Boyd, *The Middle of My Journey* (Belfast: The Blackstaff Press, 1990), 91–92.
7   Boyd, *The Middle of My Journey*, 92.

The Parochial Idyll: W. R. Rodgers

The vividness they share was projected partly as an assault on religious narrowness and cultural restriction.[8]

What influence these 'anti-puritan feelings' had on Rodgers's poetry is seen in his grasp of the difference between English and Irish poetry:

> ... the faculty of standing words or ideas on their heads – by means of pun, epigram, bull or what-have-you – is a singularly Irish one. To the English ear, which likes understatement, it is all rather excessive and therefore not in good taste. But to the Irish mind, which likes gesture, bravado, gallivanting, and rhetoric, it is an acceptable tradition.[9]

Whether or not such an 'acceptable tradition' actually exists is neither here nor there. The important thing is that Rodgers interpreted the 'Irish mind' in this, most romantic, way.

In very crude terms, the poetic side of Rodgers's nature warred with the social and cultural inheritance, while Minister Rodgers struggled to find a definite artistic identity as a poet. 'Ireland' became an imaginative home place or cultural alternative, ironically distanced from the London axis, of which Rodgers had become part, but separate, too, from the cramped provincialism of what he called the North, 'a backwater of literature out of sight of the running stream of contemporary verse'.

The poem is charged with resolving these tensions by revelling in 'a linguistic and rhythmic ebullience, a tendency to excess'. Yet, as Longley points out in his introduction, the weakest of Rodgers's poems are those that fall into this excess, becoming over-actively 'poetic' and 'Irish', with the Os, exclamation marks, and rhetoric anticipating the wilier textual play of Paul Muldoon:

> I am Ulster, my people an abrupt people
> Who like the spiky consonants in speech
> And think the soft ones cissy; who dig
> The k and t in orchestra, detect sin
> In sinfonia, get a kick out of

---

8   Michael Longley, Introduction to W. R. Rodgers, *Poems* (Oldcastle: The Gallery Press, 1993), 11.
9   Quoted in Longley, Introduction to W. R. Rodgers, *Poems*, 15.

> Tin can, fricatives, fornication, staccato talk,
> Anything that gives or takes attack,
> Like Micks, Tagues, tinkers' gets, Vatican.[10]

'Epilogue', for the never-completed *The Character of Ireland*, ends with a rare mark of self-revelation:

> And I, born to the purple passage,
> Was heir to all that Adamnation
> And hand-me-down of doom, the late comer
> To the worn-out womb.
> The apple blushed for me bellow Bellevue,
> Lagan was my Jordan, Connswater
> My washpot, and over Belfast
> I cast out my shoe.[11]

My own preference leads me to the shorter poems, such as 'Escape' rather than the operatic 'Europa and the Bull', 'Resurrection', or 'The Journey of the Magi'. As Longley points out, there is an erotic masterpiece in 'The Net' – its Elizabethan-like formality, edged with Auden, makes Rodgers a poet of real surprise and lasting joy:

> Come, make no sound, my sweet;
> Turn down the candid lamp
> And draw the equal quilt
> Over our naked guilt [.][12]

The chief characteristic of Rodgers's poetry retells a squabble with language in a fascinating early version of what has since become a major theme in Irish poetry – the self-consciousness of poets memorializing the language they write in. Voices, words, capitalized variations of both (like Humbug), mouths, silence, and galleries of abstractions like contempt, glory, imagination, and pity are the stock in Rodgers's trade. He is finding a voice pitched somewhere between the parables and anecdotes of his

---

10   Rodgers, 'Epilogue,' *Poems*, 106.
11   Rodgers, 'Epilogue,' *Poems*, 107.
12   Rodgers, 'The Net,' *Poems*, 79.

scriptural life (as a Presbyterian minister) and a free form that verbally chastises the strictness he left behind him:

> Night rounds on Europe now. And I must go
> Before its hostile faces peer and pour
> Over the mind's rim enveloping me,
> And my so-frightened thoughts dart here and there
> Like trout among the grim stony gazes.[13]

There is a great deal in Rodgers's poetry that has yet to be understood. In his writing, you sense how emblematic cultural options can take up a poet's time and get in the way of the real job that is staring him in the face. Rodgers appreciated this dilemma and this is why there is the desire in his poetry for freedom, an awakening from which he, among others, could start again, as if from the beginning.

Echoes of that yearning and rapture are found in the work of many writers and artists from a Protestant background. They are given fearsome poignancy in the revelations of Beckett, in the poetry of MacNeice and Longley, and in the music and lyrics of an artist Rodgers has probably the most in common with today, Van Morrison.

[1993]

---

13 Rodgers, 'An Irish Lake,' *Poems*, 36.

CHAPTER 10

An Unmoved Mind: John Millington Synge

I

This is the Anglo-American poet Thom Gunn introducing his selection of Ben Jonson's poetry:

> His poetry (as apart from his plays) has always been surprisingly neglected, considering its variety, and surely one reason for the neglect in the last century and a half is that so much of it can be damned as 'occasional'. That is, much of it is elicited by external events, or is intended to complement some noble, or is written to commend another person's book. And nowadays we tend to use the phrase 'occasional poetry' to indicate trivial or insincere writing.
>
> Yet in fact all poetry is occasional: whether the occasion is an external event like a birthday or a declaration of war, whether it is an occasion of the imagination, or whether it is in some sort of combination of the two.... The occasion in all cases – literal or imaginary – is the starting point, only, of a poem, but it should be a starting point to which the poet must in some sense stay true. The truer he is to it, the closer he sticks to what for him is its authenticity, the more he will be able to draw from it in the adventures that it produces, adventures that consist of the experience of writing.[1]

This longish quotation has stayed with me for two reasons. Firstly, because the quotation was very much in my mind when I was editing a selection of Synge's poetry. I had been looking forward immensely to doing so when the publishers, because of economic difficulties, had to withdraw the edition. What follows is an abbreviated version of what I might have written in that ghostly introduction. Secondly, what Thom Gunn says about Jonson holds true for Synge in interesting ways, particularly in that notion of *authenticity*. By which I do not mean verisimilitude or

---

[1] Thom Gunn, Introduction, *Ben Jonson* (Harmondsworth: Penguin, 1974), 9–10.

notions of dramatic realism. For it seems to me that one of the obsessions of Synge's life as a writer and as a man was to discover through his writing an appropriate life. Recall that famous statement he makes in the preface to *Poems and Translations*: 'Many of the older poets ... used the whole of their personal life as their material.'²

Thom Gunn's phrase is central to what I have to say about Synge's poetry: the closer the poet sticks to what for him is authentic, the more he or she will be able to draw from it (and *this* is the phrase) 'in the adventures that it produced, adventures that consist of the experience of writing'. My point is simply this: that in his poetry Synge was experimenting with formal ways to convey the immediacy of his experience. The poems dramatize his search to find an appropriate voice that could say the things he deeply felt but found difficulty in expressing directly, particularly since the conventions of his time in Ireland militated against such expression of self, the nationalist emphasis obviously being against such seemingly unfettered individualism.

Synge was, in a way, lucky because he was a stoic. Upbringing and ill-health had made him a contained and reserved man. As Yeats has it in his preface to the first edition, 1909, that most moving lament to his lost friend and obvious inspiration: '[Synge] once said to me, "We must unite asceticism, stoicism, ecstasy; two of these have often come together but not all three." '³

Synge had the ability throughout his short life to objectify his self (ascetical stoicism) and inspect his needs and desires (ecstasy). His poetry is the key to that brief life but also to his work as a dramatist; it is his shorthand. Again, Yeats's witness is important here:

> He was a solitary undemonstrative man, never asking pity, nor complaining, nor seeking but in this book's momentary cries: all folded up in brooding intellect, knowing nothing of new books and newspapers, reading the great masters alone: and he was but the more hated because he gave his country what it needed, an unmoved mind where there is a perpetual last day, a trumpeting, and calling up to judgement.⁴

2 *J. M. Synge: Collected Works Vol. I.:Poems*, ed. Robin Skelton (London: Oxford University Press, 1962), xxxvi.
3 *J. M. Synge, Collected Works Vol. I*, xxxiv.
4 *J. M. Synge, Collected Works Vol. I*, xxxv.

There is in that phrase 'an unmoved mind' a hint of the artistic inviolability that clearly Yeats admired so much in Synge.

II

Much has been made of Synge's break from the beliefs and assumptions of his family's life. In a fascinating essay, 'Synge and Heroism', Seamus Deane writes of the various 'transpositions' that Synge underwent. Synge's career, Deane points out, 'seems at first to have been dominated by a series of actual escapes and symbolic reorderings'.[5]

Most writers undergo similar transpositions. Think of Samuel Beckett, for instance, or indeed, another poet with whom I see Synge having particular affinities, Wilfred Owen. In all three cases, the individual writer struggled to discover a harsher, almost vulgarized voice in which to speak. The poems of Synge and Owen (and of Beckett too) when they had cast off defensive literary mannerisms sought to dramatize different kinds of language as speech. For Owen, the driving force of this imaginative need was his experience in the First World War, but even before this he realized the vulnerability of the artistic persona in his apprenticeship poems.

Beckett deliberately disrupted the linguistic and grammatical 'rules' of poetic form by twisting his poems into extraordinary mazes of allusion until he broke free of that showmanship and found the truer voice in poems like 'Gnome' and 'The Vulture' and in the novel cycles. Thirty years earlier, Synge, rewriting his poems of the late 1890s and, all too briefly, from 1906 writing new work, reasoned with himself about what he wanted to do in poetry. The young fugitive writer of the Paris years was confronted with the older poet's search for authenticity. It is at the very core of his preface to the *Poems and Translations*, in his letters and notebooks of the period. It is the shocking resolution of this search that Yeats understood and translated into his own work.

5   Seamus Deane, 'Synge and Heroism,' *Celtic Revivals* (London: Faber and Faber, 1985), 52.

Synge was in effect doing what poets such as Ezra Pound would demand: he was creating a tradition for himself uncompromised by the jaded poetic diction of late Victorian poetry and its Irish manifestations of the time. Synge looked through that rhetoric, even while, paradoxically, he was morally, religiously, and, perhaps, sexually bound by the curious conventions of Victorian Irish Protestantism.

The search for authenticity in writing, what Synge called 'a real literary existence', became an experience in itself. I am not talking about notions of realism or how true to life his literary creations were. Synge was instead preoccupied with the vitality of the fiction; literally, the power of the poet's voice in the poem. It was a preoccupation that drove the writer's actual life. Both became one as Yeats readily explained:

> If Synge had married young or taken some profession, I doubt if he would have written books or been greatly interested in a movement like ours; but he refused various opportunities of making money in what must have been an almost unconscious preparation. He had no life outside his imagination, little interest in anything that was not its chosen subject. He hardly seems aware of the existence of other writers. I never knew if he cared for work of mine, and do not remember that I had from him even a conventional compliment, and yet he had the most perfect modesty and simplicity in daily intercourse, self-assertion was impossible to him.[6]

This may well account for the scrupulous tensions of some of Synge's letters and comments of this time. The search took him through his own past into another world. Sometimes that world was called Ireland but it was also known as Aran, Wicklow, Kerry, Paris, and could be called Molly Allgood along with other women he cherished in his life. Here is Synge's marvellous naming of the imaginative coordinates for this emotionally dangerous yet self-possessed territory of the artist's mind: 'The strong things of life are needed in poetry ... to show that what is exalted, or tender, is not made by feeble blood. It may almost be said that before verse can be human again it must learn to be brutal.'[7]

---

6   W. B. Yeats, 'J. M. Synge and the Ireland of His Time,' *Essays and Introductions* (New York: Macmillan, 1961), 329.
7   *J. M. Synge, Collected Works Vol. I,* xxxvi.

So when Seamus Deane writes of Synge that 'before he could discover the new language or the new art he had to discover the new Ireland' and to do that, 'he had to forsake his Protestant, evangelical beliefs and attitudes', it might actually make more sense to conflate the appealing critical propriety here.[8]

Synge did not 'forsake' his Protestant past, discover a new language and art by discovering Ireland. He discovered all these things through and in the language that he had 'heard among the country people of Ireland': the spoken language (a sung language) that he wanted to convert onto the page. Consequently he imitates the bloody, brutal, and harsh; the complaints, curses, and love songs of the Irish oral tradition. Yet the proximity to the Ezra Pound of *Persona* is also unmistakable. Pound wrote a play, *The Consolation of Matrimony*, that recalls *The Playboy* and he also wrote an essay on 'John Synge and the Habits of Criticism', which took to task Maurice Bourgeois's biography of Synge.[9] We are, as is so often the case with Irish writers, looking in two directions at the same time: Synge as traditional modernist. This is Synge writing in the first draft of his preface: 'At the moment of creation the balance of the critical and creative impulses which works in the forming of any artistic production is the essential element of the writer's temperament at that moment.'[10]

Synge's poems were the purest, most vulnerable yet controlled statement of this balance. As he writes in a letter to Yeats: 'I do not at times feel sure of them [the poems], at other times I feel it would be better to print them now while I am alive, than to leave them after me to go God knows where.'[11]

Cuala finally published the book before Maunsel's trade edition. Synge never saw it in print. Worries about the size of the book, about two poems which Miss Yeats at Cuala Press considered 'too strong' ('The Curse' and 'Danny') were eventually reconciled by Yeats: 'I think this book too has certain sentences, fierce or beautiful or melancholy, that will be remembered

---

8   Deane, 'Synge and Heroism,' 51.
9   Ezra Pound, 'John Synge and the Habits of Criticism,' *Egoist*, 1:3 (2 February 1914), 53–54.
10   *J. M. Synge, Collected Works Vol. I*, xiv.
11   *J. M. Synge, Collected Works, Vol. I*, xv.

in our history, having behind their passion his quarrel with ignorance, and those passionate events, his books.'[12] *Those passionate events, his books*. They were the occasions of Synge's life and the poems he wrote were written not as doodles along the margins of his plays but as essential statements of his imaginative understanding. So what of these poems, and translations?

Of the sixty or so poems (and other material from which I am quoting) gathered together in Robin Skelton's edition of *J. M. Synge: Collected Works* (Vol. 1), excluding the twenty-five translations from Villon, Leopardi, Petrarch, and others, many of the poems in English read as translations from Irish. Synge was clearly trying to impersonate the direct form of bardic address that plays with ironic doubt, ultimate acceptance, and transcending defiance. The poems are short dramatic monologues that we entertain, listening to a tone of voice or a shifting inflection as in 'A Question':

: I asked if I got sick and died, would you

With my black funeral go walking too,
If you'd stand close to hear them talk or pray
While I'm let down in that steep bank of clay.

And, No, you said, for if you saw a crew
Of living idiots, pressing round that new
Oak coffin – they alive, I dead beneath
That board, – you'd rave and rend them with your teeth.

As has been remarked so often in Synge's dramatic work, the merging of death with passion recurs in his poetry as well:

You are a peasant, mere maid by the day,
Humming in Gaelic sad songs while you dust,
I am a passer on paths of grey,
With a wallet half-worn for rhymes and a crust.

You who have eyes like stars lost in a wave.
A cadence to challenge dim nights of cold,
I think you lean to my chant of the grave,
Will weave with my passion wild web for a shroud.
　　　　　'The Serving Girl'

12　*J. M. Synge, Collected Works, Vol. I*, xxxiii.

An Unmoved Mind: John Millington Synge

The poems haunt gravesides and ruins, experience bodily decay and disease, while in the very same breath they speak of spring, dawns, and the bounty of nature. But to establish a thematic network might prove tedious, given the exactness of these poems and what I can only call their lack of pretension. There is, however, a concentration at their source, a musical focus that is revealed in Synge's sense of his poems as forming a sequence. (Editorially, it may make more sense to number these poems in the manner of Emily Dickinson's work.) The focus consists of several distinctive elements: the identifiable landscape, the fugitive, often plaintive, voice, and the inevitable refrain of a life passing. That said, I think also of Synge's 'city' poems, when he collects a bright incidental moment and generalizes from it, as in 'Notre Dame de Champs'.

> Pigeons are cooing along the eaves
> Grey flies are wooing their like on the leaves;
>
> White-hood sisters sit at their prayer
> With dronings that beat at my breast with the air;
>
> The dust and the pavement are hot to my skin,
> 'Rise, little sisters, and let me in,
>
> 'You who are fragrant, and cool, and white,
> Sisters of Mercy, to love is delight!'

The aphoristic compression of these last four words, 'to love is delight', runs alongside the imagistic 'Winter' as the twin tracks of Synge's poetic desire. Again, we are faced with the isolated, forlorn speaking voice as if it were a singer's voice:

> There's snow in every street
> Where I go up and down,
> And there's no woman, man, or dog
> That knows me in the town.

What complicates this picture, and indeed deepens it, is Synge's obvious pleasure in mimicking the ballad form: take a look at 'A Mountain Creed (Ballad of a Pauper)', 'Patch-Shaneen', and 'Danny'. Synge also wrote at least two songs in 'On an Island' and 'Beg-Innish'. It is interesting to compare the latter with W. H. Auden's song 'Master and Boatswain'. There is also the lusty 'Queens' and the partially successful street song, or recitation, 'The 'Mergency Man'. For in the diversity of these poems, Synge's impersonation of other voices and styles of address are heavily mannered but entirely convincing such as in 'Queens' where the mix of learning and colloquial idiom is straight out of the Irish traditional songbook. But the stylistic range of Synge's poetry should not distract us from their core value, which is to be found in his attempt to fabricate adventure. This is what Synge meant when he wrote that 'the strong things of life are needed in poetry'. He believed, if I read him correctly, that poetry, or language itself, could re-create those 'strong things' – passion, death, laughter, joy. The real romance in Synge's life was the adventure in creating these 'things' as language.

It was an ambition also full of the moral contradiction that Synge anticipated in a disturbing phrase: 'Before verse can be human again it must learn to be brutal.' Brutality does not enter into his poems, but the poems are conditioned by the brutal reality of death and Synge's defiant sense of what this adds up to in 'A Word on the Life-Force':

> You squirrel angel eel and bat
> You seal, sea-serpent water-hen
> You badger cur-dog mule and cat
> You player with the shapes of men

I can think of no more chilling poem in modern English that presents the reader with the incontrovertible truth of existence as the little poem 'End of the Book' that ends Robin Skelton's edition:

> I read about the Blaskets and Dunquin,
> The Wicklow towns and fair days I've been in.
> I read of Galway, Mayo, Aranmore,
> And men with kelp along a wintry shore.
> Then I remembered that that 'I' was I,
> And I'd a filthy job – to waste and die.

It is the kind of poem we would like to laugh at; since, in what he called his 'grimmer verse', Synge could always call upon humour. A bleak, black humour that is so much a part of his drama too. The energy of his poems, however, holds them back from self-pity in precisely the same way that Irish songs achieve this subtle balance. Reading them over again, one thinks of Synge's poetry as crucial experiments in which he was exploring his self, finding out who and what he was. That this identity had much to do with the cultural and religious influences of his past is obvious and unmistakable. What is not so clear is that the identity Synge was forging in these poems grew out of the stoic aloneness, that 'solitary undemonstrative' nature that Yeats, amongst others, found so impregnable and alluring, at the same time. It was an artistic persona rare in twentieth-century Irish writing where writers are first seen as great characters and entertainers, identified by the crudest forms of stereotypes, rather than by their writing. Synge's contradiction was in resisting that enticement while being drawn to the cultural and moral energies that underpin it. To me, as a young student moving out of a northern, Protestant, urban background, encountering the west of Ireland and writing poems, Synge was a kind of role model. There is about his poems, as there was about the man himself, the clear-sighted integrity of an artist who is preoccupied with the exact and exacting experience of writing, rather than the hoo-ha of being a writer. As he wrote with magisterial understatement in one of his notebooks: '[W]e need not expect to say anything very new but in applying for ourselves to our own life what is thought in different ways by many we [are] likely to hit on matters of some value.'[13]

[1994]

---

13   J. M. Synge, *Collected Works, Vol. I*, xiv.

CHAPTER 11

Our Secret Being: Padraic Fiacc

I

Padraic Fiacc has been publishing for almost fifty years. The unmistakable shape and sound of his poems have found a lasting artistic echo in the personal and social traumas of his own life and times. That this poetry radically subverts what we often expect to see and hear in a poem is clear from the outset of *Ruined Pages: Selected Poems of Padraic Fiacc*.[1] The collection is intended to serve as an introduction to Fiacc's work – from the earliest surviving poems of the 1940s to those of the present – and also includes 'Hell's Kitchen', Fiacc's account of the autobiographical and cultural sources of his writing.

The poetry of Padraic Fiacc departs from the Gaelic otherworld of myth and folklore before settling in the uncharted territory that is Belfast's violent history. It is a story told with fantastic realism and melodramatic relish. Fiacc's work is preoccupied with language as a physically despoiled body – the violated page, the exploded word order. There has been much talk of late about the theme of inner exile and the use of dialect as a means of refurbishing the jaded artistic persona and poetic of contemporary literature in English. Here, too, Fiacc's work is central, for no figure of the Poet could be more isolated and more aware of the fact than Fiacc himself, while his poems are obsessed with the actual word-ordering and depth-charge nuances of common speech.

---

1   Padraic Fiacc, *Ruined Pages: Selected Poems of Padraic Fiacc*, eds. Gerald Dawe and Aodán Mac Póilin (Belfast: The Blackstaff Press, 1994). All quotations in this chapter are to poems in this edition.

Fiacc's ability to use idiomatic phrasing and cliché is a marvellous illustration of one of his poetry's main values. Similarly, the voice that in 'A Slight Hitch' describes the 'ghost-faced boy-broadcaster' who breaks down '(can you imagine, and him / 'live' on the TV screen!)' is drawn against 'the usual cold, acid / and dignified way' of the (capitalized) 'NORTHERN IRELAND BRITISH/ BROADCASTING CORPORATION'.[2] This linguistic battle for authenticity, at the very heart of Fiacc's poetry, aligns him with the work of Tony Harrison and other 'Barbarian' poets of today. It is a verbal dexterity paralleled by the imagery of his poetry. Read the opening of 'More Terrorists':

> The prayer book is putting on fat
> With *in memoriam* cards.
>
> The dead steal back
> Like snails on the draining board
>
> Caught after dark
> Out of their shells.[3]

Throughout Fiacc's work the pervasive sense of childhood (of the poet's own childhood, of his daughter's, and, in a bizarre way, of the entire city's) cuts up against the deadly inheritance of sectarian hatred and violence, 'crossing our stunted lives', as he writes in 'Glass Grass'.[4] It is the ordinary lives that are stripped of stability and forced instead to live with fear:

> Then the lamp was hurled
> And geranium pot after geranium pot
> Before whoever it was could
> Find her a bed in the asylum from
> Childhood to childhood, in a world
> – womb to womb: to womb removed.[5]

---

2   Fiacc, *Ruined Pages*, 117.
3   Fiacc, *Ruined Pages*, 64.
4   Fiacc, *Ruined Pages*, 129.
5   Fiacc, *Ruined Pages*, 139.

This comes from 'Dark Night of the Mill Hag' and there are other similar portraits, like the Kafkaesque 'Dirty Protest', which asks how life ever became so broken: 'Blown up, thrown down born alive.'[6]

The intellectual legacy that shadows Fiacc's poetry draws from a Catholic education, turned on its head and spliced with modernism, as Pascal, Mauriac, Baudelaire, and Joyce coalesce in Fiacc's troubled imagination. There is, too, a wry, terse, almost despairing humour reminiscent of John Berryman, as in 'Intimate Letter 1973':

> Our Paris part of Belfast has
> Decapitated lamp posts now. Our meeting
> Place, the Book Shop, is a gaping
> Black hole of charred timber.[7]

Fiacc can blend these poetic skills into a beautiful poignant lyric, such as 'Goodbye to Brigid / *an Agnus Dei*', with its opening evocation of Belfast offering up the unforgettable plea:

> My little girl, my Lamb of God,
> I'd like to set you free from
> Bitch Belfast as we pass the armed
>
> -to-the-back-teeth barracks and
> Descend the road into the school
> Grounds of broken windows from
>
> A spate of car-bombs, but
> Don't forgive me for not.[8]

II

Padraic Fiacc's poetry traces his imagination's troubled and broken course through the impounding claims of Irish history and mythology.

---

6   Fiacc, *Ruined Pages*, 146.
7   Fiacc, *Ruined Pages*, 119.
8   Fiacc, *Ruined Pages*, 118.

Chronologically *Ruined Pages* charts Fiacc's engagement with both these forces, a process marked by personal idealism, and then disillusionment that finally breaks down, recoiling from any such 'logic', withdrawing from possibility itself into the 'depths of our dark / Secret being'[9] ('Credo Credo').

Up to and including 'First Movement', the poems from Fiacc's first published collection, *By the Black Stream*, are written with a clear conception of the Irish monastic style.[10] Sharp syntactical inversions, bright colours, and sense of the world as a natural wonder against which man is a sort of tragicomic intrusion: these traditional features conceal the stolen joy of the poet.

These innocent perceptions seem to exist in spite of the encroaching strain of the world, of experience threatening to stain the poet's consciousness, and it is here that the jagged thrust of Fiacc's imagery takes over. 'Der Bomben Poet 1941' strangely anticipates Fiacc's poetic fate in this regard. The more disharmonious nature is seen to be, the more discordant and unpredictable the world, the more the poet tries to cast images in chaotic likeness, as in 'The Ghost':

> Out of bull resentment
> Snores to the moon
> At black nightfall
>
> By my side a skull
> Hunted Dermot down:
>
> In all the land the lack
> Of what was whole.[11]

Poems like 'Master Clay', 'Lives of a Student', 'Themes from a Gloss', and 'Alive O' are tuned into each other. This complementary process becomes disturbed and disjointed, however, at quite an early point, as in 'First Movement'. Fiacc is obviously aware of the importance of this poem

---

9   Fiacc, *Ruined Pages*, 141.
10 Padraic Fiacc, *By the Black Stream* (Dublin: The Dolmen Press, 1969).
11 Fiacc, *Ruined Pages*, 61.

since he has brought it into two collections, marking points of hesitancy and anticipation of change. The poem is also noticeable for its accomplished simplicity and the characteristic contrasting of urban with natural imagery:

> I was born on such a morning
> Smelling of the Bone Yards
>
> The smoking chimneys over the slate rooftops
> The wayward storm birds

But the following passage is particularly relevant here:

> And to the east where morning is, the sea
> And to the west where evening is, the sea
>
> Threatening with danger
>
> And it would always darken suddenly.[12]

That sudden darkening and threatening with danger is the first key perception that Fiacc makes of his disintegrating relationship with the world around him. 'First Movement' demonstrates the characteristic style in which Fiacc's poems circle to the source of danger and threat; stunned by the sudden eruption of buried energies and forces that obliterate danger (which is immanent, an exposure to harm) with the deluge of reality. It is for this uncompromising recognition that Fiacc is best known, as he wryly says in 'Glass Grass': 'My fellow poets call my poems 'cryptic, crude, dis/-tasteful, brutal, savage, bitter ....'[13]

The tempestuous reputation that is all too often associated with Fiacc's poetry is deduced from the 'brutal, savage, bitter'. Such a reading is one-sided because it fails to account for the sources of Fiacc's poetry, or to describe the technical skills he brings to his writing.

---

12 Fiacc, *Ruined Pages*, 75.
13 Fiacc, *Ruined Pages*, 131.

The general impression given by Fiacc's work is one of entrapment: man is held in a painful stasis, pinned between the past and the future and, in this vision, images drawn from religion and impoverished social conditions coalesce. One of the most powerful physical images of this stasis can be found in 'Internee':

> And it does not hurt
> To be jeered at
>
> When you are hanging
> Upside down.
>
> When hanging upside down hurts more.[14]

Fiacc's own experience of Ireland as the conflict between an ideal world and terrible reality is a persistent theme in his poetry. In 'Icon' Ireland is the cause and effect of the individual's entrapment:

> Unholy mother Ireland banging
> on the wall in labour.
>
> We were born in her
>
> Screams to 'Get Out!'[15]

But if Ireland is seen as a mother giving birth, in 'Fire Light' the life given is interpreted with existential despair:

> … in this so strange
> 'So Be It Now' as if
>
> It never really were
> Or never will be.
>
> Only always is.[16]

---

14   Fiacc, *Ruined Pages*, 145.
15   Fiacc, *Ruined Pages*, 97–98.
16   Fiacc, *Ruined Pages*, 102.

Fiacc constantly stresses an enclosed, trapped world; one where 'We all run away from each other's / Particular hell' ('Intimate Letter 1973')[17] and the force that superintends the hell has an absolute stature in 'Our Father': 'The evil thing being/That which crushes us.'[18] Fiacc rarely attempts to overcome the darkness, but in 'The Fall' he makes the gesture of rebellion:

> It's vengeance I want
> But vengeance on whom?[19]

It is as if Fiacc refuses to acknowledge this life; our being is corrupt, and his poetry speaks of the disintegrated ontology we have inherited with all its vast psychic (as much as social) injustice. But if Fiacc's work operates on this level in general, the poems deal with specific and identifiable onrushes of reality: the oppressive 'military machine', the deprived environment of a discarded working class, or the impact of mythology on everyday life, as in 'Elegy in 'the Holy Land'':

> O Dolly-Eurydice, my dark Ros
> – aleen dream
> of bog on bog of bone
> – grounded cloud, Ireland, my dear
>
> Dragon seed pod.[20]

Most poignantly, this sense of failure resides in family life, where the contradiction between dream and reality is most acute, as in the imagery of 'Goodbye to Our Father':

> I see your bone-naked
> Face scrutinising 'Injustices' still!
>
> Never bother! You have a hole to hide in now.[21]

---

17 Fiacc, *Ruined Pages*, 119.
18 Fiacc, *Ruined Pages*, 94.
19 Fiacc, *Ruined Pages*, 78.
20 Fiacc, *Ruined Pages*, 114.
21 Fiacc, *Ruined Pages*, 95.

If there is no release from the entrapment, if there are no ways out, Fiacc can see the black humour of being there. He does this through self-dramatization and by the use of the aggressive understatements of Belfast vernacular speech. Fiacc's poetry deals with the urban landscape and in this he separates himself again from the general drift of Irish poetry. With its bases in rural landscapes – decayed, mythic, or desolate – and its metaphoric wells sunk far from 'the damp down by the half-dried river / Slimy at night on the mud flats' ('Haemorrhage'),[22] Irish poetry has tended to evade the city as imaginatively hostile or indifferent. In 'The Black and the White' Fiacc strikes the exact note of city life, the hostility is embraced, the empty night-time streets, the loneliness, violence, and loss:

> Sinking on iron street, the bin-lid
> -shielded, battleship-grey-faced kids
>
> Shinny up the lamp post, cannot tear
> Themselves away, refuse to come in
>
> From the dying lost day.[23]

It is not that city life is a contagion; in 'Our Fathers' it is infected by industrial wastefulness:

> A grey cloud of pollution from Power
> Chimneys, mill house, laundries, cars.[24]

When this environment is born of a corrupting past, the violent present spreads through every perception, affecting it with inevitable meaning that imposes itself, like the remorseless rain, on our consciousness, as in 'The Wrong Ones':

> The howl of the rain beating on the military tin
> Roof is like the tolling of a bell
> Tolling for a childhood more

22   Fiacc, *Ruined Pages*, 81.
23   Fiacc, *Ruined Pages*, 109.
24   Fiacc, *Ruined Pages*, 46.

> Murdering than murdered.
>
> I rise and stalk across the scarred with storm
> -erected daisies, night in the north, grass.[25]

Throughout Fiacc's poetry, and in his past commentaries upon it and upon literature in general, there runs a deep hostility to the paraphernalia of art.

Fiacc's Beckettian anti-art abandon caustically overthrows, so to speak, the pretentiousness of art, while cauterizing the poet's own unavoidable and reckless bonds with life. Fiacc's sense of himself as a poet is, accordingly, both mocking and tragic. The often ugly, parasitic relationship between literature and its immediate or historical world of suffering can, in Fiacc's book, lead to a neutralizing of that suffering. Literature seems to stabilize the violence by drawing it into its own circuit of imaginative ordering. In the lived world the suffering continues to overwhelm. Such ambiguities cannot be left out of the picture because they are part of the imaginative process: to excise them damages and destroys the terrible truthfulness that Fiacc's poetry struggles to articulate, for his poems dramatize the human effects of moral and psychological decay upon the lives of the ordinary people for whom, and from whom, he speaks. Time after time his poetry points to the erosion of human potential, and the indictment is laid at the door of the political establishment. No other poet writing in Ireland today has been so forthright and committed to saying the uncomfortable thing. Padraic Fiacc is the first of Belfast's poets to have imaginatively possessed, with such unremitting intensity, not only his own life, but also the life of his profoundly troubled city. It is an extraordinary, disturbing achievement.

[1994]

---

25 Fiacc, *Ruined Pages*, 136.

CHAPTER 12

Breathing Spaces: Brendan Kennelly

> There is no audience in Ireland, though I have managed to build up out of my head a little audience for myself. The real problem is the scarcity of a right audience which draws out of a poet what is best in him. The Irish audience that I came in contact with tried to draw out of me everything that was loud, journalistic and untrue.[1]

I

Much of what Brendan Kennelly has written is influenced, directly or indirectly, by the problem so boldly stated by Patrick Kavanagh in his *Self-Portrait* quoted above. In particular, Kennelly's early poems, most of which are collected in the volume *Breathing Spaces*,[2] chart his growing unease and concern with making what he simply calls 'connection': 'The sense of connection, when it occurs, feels like a stroke of great good luck. But with whom or what does it become even momentarily possible to connect?'[3] The need, to quote Kavanagh again, 'to build up ... a little audience for myself' is taken over by Kennelly as both a personal and a cultural mission. Kennelly's poetry inhabits the artistic ground where these two impulses collide.

Undoubtedly this provocative intersection accounts for the extraordinary commitment Brendan Kennelly has shown during the 1980s to give readings from his work, primarily throughout Ireland, but also abroad. It

---

1   Patrick Kavanagh, *Self-Portrait* (Dublin: The Dolmen Press, 1963), 14.
2   The poetry and prose quoted in this chapter are taken from Brendan Kennelly, *Breathing Spaces: Early Poems* (Newcastle-upon-Tyne: Bloodaxe Books, 1992).
3   Kennelly, *Breathing Spaces*, 129.

may also account for his willingness to speak on various moral and sexual issues that emerged in the country throughout the same period.

This high-profile public persona was consummated in Kennelly's book-length poems, or epics, *Cromwell* and *The Book of Judas*, and has certainly contributed enormously to his vast popular reputation in Ireland.

In the earlier work, such as *Love Cry* (1972), *Islandman* (1977), *A Small Light* (1979), *A Girl* (1981), and in the previously uncollected poems gathered in the title section, *Breathing Spaces*, one sees the extent to which Kennelly has been preoccupied with these polemical issues of audience and the poet's place in a society such as Ireland – so very traditional in ways, and yet brashly, almost aggressively, engaged with the new.

What makes *Breathing Spaces* particularly revealing is that, in the introduction and notes accompanying each section of the book, Kennelly alludes to a deep anxiety about the fault lines that run between the traditional, community life in Ireland and its demise. It is an anxiety Kavanagh would have well understood.

In a sense, Kennelly is to the Republic of the 1980s what Kavanagh was to the Republic of the 1940s and 1950s. Both poets are haunted by bardic nostalgia; both suspicious of highbrow pretensions about 'Art'; both are mindful of the subversiveness of the comic spirit and both respect the rhetorical wisdom of anecdote and folklore. Indeed, while much has been made of Seamus Heaney's intellectual appropriation of Kavanagh's example, we should bear in mind the equally important cultural similarities that Brendan Kennelly shares with Kavanagh.

To take even the most obvious of examples: both poets come from a small-town/rural village background, the familiarity of which led to a sense of spiritual shock and personal difficulty when confronted by city life. This breakdown is recorded in the poems with pathos, bitterness, and, sometimes, self-mockery.

Kavanagh's distaste for Dublin's literary life is legendary. 'I wasted what could have been my four glorious years', Kavanagh recalls in *Self-Portrait*, 'begging and scrambling around the streets of malignant Dublin.'

The experience of leaving behind the known, identifiable world of Inniskeen for Dublin in 1939, and the kind of personal distortions and loss that this change seems to have brought about in Kavanagh's psyche, is a dominant theme in his poetry. It is the focus for *Self-Portrait* and provides the radical poignancy to Kavanagh's life and work as a poet:

> Round about the late nineteen thirties a certain prosperity came through and foolishly enough that was the time I chose to leave my native fields. I had no messianic impulse to leave. I was happy. I went against my will. A lot of our actions are like that. We miss the big emotional gesture and drift away. Is it possible to achieve our potential grand passion? I believe so. Perhaps that has been my weakness.[4]

Kavanagh's Monaghan provided him with what he called 'the right simplicity' that he had to rediscover ('back to where I started') in order to achieve 'weightlessness' – the unforced, indifferent mystery that is the hallmark of true poetry.

The Kerry and Shannon where Kennelly grew up during the late 1930s, 1940s, and early 1950s provide him with rich local detail, landscape, stories, and the very simplicity of language that characterizes *Breathing Spaces*.

Like Kavanagh, Kennelly records the transition of the individual from having a defined and definite place in a community, to another world of broken and fractured identities wherein 'the self' is effectively unknowable in the received and hierarchic terms of the parish. The self becomes, instead, the site of 'egotism', a deeply suspect force in Kennelly's lexicon.

Kennelly's uncertainty in addressing the self is matched by Kavanagh's reticence: 'I dislike talking about myself in a direct way. The self is only interesting as an illustration' is how Kavanagh opens his *Self-Portrait*. Similarly, Kennelly states in his note to *Islandman*:

> Through an act of sustained and deliberate indirectness, it is possible to say more completely whatever one has to say. It is one of the fertile paradoxes of poetry that one can be more candid by engaging less in frontalism and by listening more keenly to the voices of the personae in the wings.[5]

Throughout his introduction and in the notes to the individual volumes of *Breathing Spaces*, Kennelly is troubled by 'the self'. It is a 'mobile,

---

4   Kavanagh, *Self-Portrait*, 10–11.
5   Kennelly, *Breathing Spaces*, 102.

boggy swamp of egotism and dull confusion' – a phrase that he repeats – and he refers later to the 'monstrous yet magnificent energies of egotism'. Other references include the *mere* self, the *messy* self, all by way of disentangling the one moral and artistic problem that Kennelly clearly sees as being paramount to his own identity as a writer: 'I sometimes think that poetry takes the mickey out of poets. The problem is to keep the egolife from mauling the poemlife.' Indeed, poetry threatens to become a *substitute* for the self, an alternative life almost, which bridges the past, and its known community (an inherited audience, in effect), with the present, atomized reality.

Many of the poems in *Breathing Spaces* literally document, sociologically, anthropologically, the traditional community, as in *Love Cry*, a sequence of forty sonnets. The poems name a place or person, tell stories, and relate the passing of a way of life. It is poetry as lament. While conscious of the brute realities of farming, Kennelly dramatizes the beauty of the landscape wherein his 'characters' live out their lives. Little is gone into, but the sufficient exterior of *Love Cry* reveals a terrifying cycle of acceptance, tinged with regret and, often, curtailed rage, as in 'Spring' which opens:

> Curtin spent the winter in the County Home
> And drank and whored and gambled in the spring;
> I met him once, the black days coming on,
> He told me straight that he was going in.
> 'Last night', he said, 'I left a farmer's house,
> The moon was up, a wicked light abroad,
> The innocent roads were turning treacherous
> And ice, you know, is the pure cruelty of God.

The poem displays the characteristic attributes of *Breathing Spaces*: the encounter, the conversation, the voice, the closure of the concluding last line – 'And then – the spring!' What is so noticeable about *Breathing Spaces* is the extent to which the poems, ranging over twenty years, are shadowed by death, pain, and loss.

It is as if, deprived of the defined communal world, the poet finds recompense in the language and social conditions of the past, only to realize that these no longer exist and that the world view they embody has fragmented and is, effectively, dead. How else is one to account for the (almost) obsessive preoccupation of the poems with death, dying, ghosts, and the adequacy of poetry to convey such experience?

> The fields were strewn with dead metaphors.
> Language had fought a pitched battle and lost.

Physical death is omnipresent in *Breathing Spaces*. There is too the notion that failure, as another form of death, must be acknowledged by the poetic imagination, since nothing should be repugnant to the poet. 'Failure is your daily bread.' 'It is the source / of all our celebration', as Kennelly remarks in 'Failure', concluding the poem:

> I will look at all this, loving it
> As I have always loved it,
> Feeling the failure rise like the tide,
> Waves wasting their perfection
> On my ignorant shores.

So the poet becomes an icon of authentic life, taking everything 'in' and by that very fact celebrating life in the teeth of denial, repression, and insufficiency. This late-Romantic notion, conditioned by the joking, devilish quality in the poetic personae, finds straightforward endorsement in Kennelly's introductory note to 'Islandman':

> I want to love every heartbeat, every musical second of happiness and grief, boredom and fun and the usual no-man's-land of viable and reasonably rewarded half-being, permitted between stoneself and definitive dust. Whatever forces help one to love this frequently muted music of time are to be welcomed by imagination and intelligence, body and soul. Whatever or whoever you are, be with me now.[6]

The yearning here ('be with me now') does have a religious dimension to it because poetry becomes a form of secular mass, compensating for the deadliness of institutional spirituality. Kennelly's poetry, after all, depicts the lives of the victims of the Irish Catholic Church. Such failure hangs like a cultural fate against which the characters of Kennelly's poems sometimes rail, mock, but often accept with inarticulate cries from the heart.

6   Kennelly, *Breathing Spaces*, 103.

> Ritchie screamed to see his chastised son
>
> So changed, as though the quick rebuke
> Had driven him to a world unknown.
> But now he lay there, still, beyond all pain;
> The village watched and wept while Ritchie shook,
> Two women pressed eager lips upon
> Blue lips, giving their kiss of life. In vain.

In this sense, then, the poet is looked to as a figure who can strike back, if symbolically, at the forces of moral, sexual, and political containment: 'Ireland', Kennelly writes in his introduction 'is, above all, the land of the label, a green kingdom of clichés. To write poetry is to declare war on labels and clichés.' The poem is a coded message that confirms in the reader's (or audience's) mind that the poet knows what is going on, because he has suffered the same kind of repression as his audience. The poem is a vehicle of this identification. Such knowledge is not, however, absolute and incontrovertible. As Kennelly remarks in the headnote to *Love Cry*:

> I showed some of these poems to an old man from the place in which most of the poems are set. He read them and said vehemently, 'Lies! Lies! Poetry is all bloody lies!' He paused, then added, much more gently, 'But a poet's lies can make a man look twice at himself and the world'.[7]

What Kennelly has achieved in the poems of *Breathing Spaces* is to keep an accessible channel of communication open between himself and the wider public in whose name his poems are written. He has *re-created* that audience in the image of what they once were and he has been able to maintain this relationship by exploiting the language of church ritual and common speech with total ease.

> I touch the stones.
> My mother smiles, my father dances,
> My daughter peppers me with questions,
> A swimmer finds his music, an ambulance screams

---

[7] Kennelly, *Breathing Spaces*, 80.

> In mercy, I build a bridge of love,
> The willow speaks, the lightning dreams,
>
> The blackbird sings, I make a wish, the gift appears
> To bless this art
>   that deepens friendship
>   through the years.

The force of poetic personality, the telling accent of the spoken line, has meant that Kennelly's poems are essentially available as stories. In this he has kept faith with his forebears, a loyalty that marks almost every poem in *Breathing Spaces* and the ideological commitment that Kennelly declares in 'A Small Light': 'Today the idea of community is vanishing fast; what we witness for the most part, in the efforts of those who try to create them, are, however admirable the impulses behind the efforts, sad parodies of community.'[8]

Kennelly's poetry is painfully aware of the parody and the unavoidable reality that the idea of community that he re-imagines in his writing is literally *vanishing*. What exactly the idea of that community is will provide historians and cultural critics with a tantalizing glimpse of an Ireland that might have been; elusively present in the voices, feelings, and attitudes of Kennelly's country folk, 'the personae in the wings'. For all the brash rhetoric and ebullience of *Breathing Spaces,* there is a Lorca-like recognition of darkness and death and an anger at the modern world:

> Is the contemporary poet, by definition, a part-timer, one who with a grateful sign settles down to try to write when the fierce trivialities have for the moment been coped with? He is so often a voice without an audience, an endured oddity, an articulate freak with oddball values, a stone, a severed head, a voice in a void.[9]

This is plain as a pikestaff and it lays down Kennelly's just claim to be considered alongside those other poets in these islands, such as Tony Harrison, who attempt to restore the poet to some kind of public life.

Certainly Kennelly's unflagging energy in producing poetry that is popular (in the sense of being directed at the people) underlines his critical

8   Kennelly, *Breathing Spaces,* 128.
9   Kennelly, *Breathing Spaces,* 129.

relationship with Patrick Kavanagh. As Kavanagh remarked in one of the finest passages of *Self-Portrait*: 'I had been assailing the myth of Ireland by which they were managing to beat the artistic rap. I had seen and shewn that this Ireland thing was an undignified business – the trade of enemies and failures.'[10]

In the major poems that followed the collections gathered in *Breathing Spaces*, Brendan Kennelly assails 'the myth of Ireland' with a vengeance. The anticipations, echoes, and soundings that one hears in *Love Cry, A Small Light,* or 'Shelley in Dublin' are, in retrospect, unmistakable preparations for the war of words, the operatic thunder and 'fabulous fact' of Kennelly's greatest poetic achievements to date – *Cromwell* and *The Book of Judas*.

[1994]

---

10   Kavanagh, *Self-Portrait*, 18.

NICHOLAS ALLEN

Afterword

Irish poets are frequent prose writers; the essay form carries a particular charge of direct intervention in a society conscious of its continuing considerations of identity and belonging. The active agency of prose allows for immediate commentary on the writer's situation, to his or her time and place; as times change, and places with them, a collection of that prose allows us to trace the growth of imagination in the world that forms it. The collection becomes a cartography, its coordinates individual, its origins social; hence, *Northern Windows/ Southern Stars* reflects upon Gerald Dawe's own impulse to write in volatile environments, from the northern Troubles to the Celtic Tiger. Responding to these challenges required a determination to negotiate, and that negotiation continues, most importantly, between the writer and his fellows, the living and the dead who populate our imaginations.

The treaties made with these shades form the basis for critical reflection in Dawe's critical writing, situated in the evolving context of a changing Ireland in post-war Europe. That Europe has its own histories of conflict and recovery, which suggests a possible connection between the traumas of imperial decline, from Belfast to Bucharest, and composition.

Dawe's own journey into these complex pasts, his own account of the forces that found his perspective, have been charted in several books, including *The Wrong Country* (2018) and *The Sound of the Shuttle* (2020). Each of the twelve essays included in *Northern Windows/Southern Stars* debates the nature of reputation, responsibility, representation; each exploration is bound to the next by a necessity to record events as Dawe sees them, to make full account of the lives he has imagined. Movement is the key motif, the movement of mortality, that life and death of worlds imagined as artists take their brief stage to pass (and all writing, as Margaret

Atwood describes it, is a 'risky trip to the Underworld ... to bring something or someone back from the dead').¹ Dipping in an Irish Styx, Thomas Kinsella captures the fragility of this mission in 'Touching the River':

> Rivery moment, clay-fresh;
> light murmuring over the surface
> as we kneel on the brink and drive our stare
> down, now, into the current.
> Our unstopped flesh and senses
> – how they vanish!²

Like Kinsella's poem, Dawe's prose writing is a fragile buttress, a formal support to those murmuring worlds that inform Dawe's critical perception.³ Hidden as essays, reviews, and all those temporal commissions that make for a public life in any career, in literature or otherwise, Dawe's critical writing provides an echo chamber, a testing ground for new ideas that are an account of one individual's reckoning, of one writer's life.

That life was formed, in the first part, in the city of Belfast, as Dawe grew up in the northern quarters of the 1950s and early 1960s, in a mixed community of class, creed, and belief, of Christian and Jew as much as Protestant and Catholic, of redbrick houses and tidy streets. From the start, we can imagine the simple poetry of place and time having an effect on the young mind; Dawe first attended Seaview Primary school, before graduating to Orangefield in East Belfast in 1963. Both schools' names suggest a certain perspective, the primary looking to a Belfast Lough that opened out to a wider world of ships and trade, Orangefield a vision of the tropics in a climate whose main heat came from social unrest. Both names suggest hope, of better places, better times. That desire surfaces as memory in Dawe's later descriptions of 'Travels':

> the seashore rhododendrons,
> the waving bougainvillea,

---

1 Margaret Atwood, *Negotiating with the Dead. A Writer on Writing* (Cambridge: Cambridge University Press, 2002), 157.
2 Thomas Kinsella, 'Touching the River,' *Collected Poems, 1956–2001* (Manchester: Carcanet, 2001).
3 The phrase is Derek Mahon's.

> the coiling cable of the night-light,
> a fleet of spiders and ants;
>
> and the mascara'd finch
> dancing along the flowering wall.⁴

Orangefield was, in Dawe's time there, a radical experiment, an attempt to provide enlightened education to a generation of schoolchildren without previous opportunity. It worked. After school, and a short spell in London, Dawe entered the new University of Ulster at Coleraine. His three years there

> ... did not last long. They were intense though. Everything was – sitting in the campus listening to the news about the Abercorn blast, watching the slow dismantling of Belfast and the places where we used to meet *back home*.⁵

Which might make us conclude that the Troubles, that period of communal violence and sustained disintegration that erupted, but did not begin, in 1968 in the north of Ireland, were of crucial influence on the young writer. Which they were. But perhaps better to say that Dawe's own personal sense of dislocation, of fragility even, was confirmed by the Troubles, not created by it. One of his very first published poems, '… I'm through', which appeared in a little magazine called *Lines*, from the north of England, reflects upon the dying moment:

> It always happens like this
> I was told.
> First a pain, then a dagger
> And then the room closes in …
> There are women in bronze
> Painted gold, swaying and smiling to me
> And men in steel and iron
> Looking like the moon.⁶

That final estrangement, 'Looking like the moon', reminds of Padraic Fallon's estimation of the later poetry of William Butler Yeats, where Fallon

---

4   Gerald Dawe, 'Travels,' *The Morning Train* (Oldcastle: Gallery, 1999), 48.
5   Gerald Dawe, 'A Citizen of Sorts,' *Fortnight*, 24 June 1985, 15. Boston College MS 5/3.
6   Gerald Dawe, '… I'm Through,' *Lines*, 5. Boston College MS 2/5.

found Yeats 'awaken in this midnight, the coldness of the moon about him, his mind, once a disc reflecting a land of sun, now a very moon-metal turning in dark and light'.[7] Throughout, that sense of strangeness never wears off, driven by an energy, unbidden, but present regardless, that Elizabeth Bishop observed elsewhere: 'The tumult in the heart' that 'keeps asking questions'.[8]

All of which signals a development from *Krino*, the literary magazine that Dawe founded in 1986 with the late Irish language activist and scholar Aodán Mac Póilin and Avril Forrest, the aim 'to underline the European contexts of writing in Ireland'.[9] Appropriately, Dawe's reflections on Irish Literature are often cast in contexts to which we are not accustomed, such as Czeslaw Milosz's haunting observation that a 'first stroll along a street littered with glass from bomb-shattered windows, shakes your faith in the 'naturalness" of the world.[10] Dawe felt this shock, having been caught in a bombing, a year after which he and several of his friends involved had left Belfast. That Belfast vernacular, which insulated sensitivity from atrocity, a cloak made from the materials of hymnal, blues, the jazz clubs and the guttural, that substance of rapture, which fed the disparate, from W. R. Rodgers to Van Morrison, failed:

> Lord, I am far gone.
> The castle at Carrick dissolved into thin air.
> Who's stepping ashore this time –
> King Billy's horse munching hay
> or a load of guns off some cranky trawler?
>
> There's us, anyway, full as kites,
> pissing up against the restored battlements.[11]

---

7   Padraic Fallon, 'Review of *The Winding Stair and Other Poems*,' *Dublin Magazine*, April–June 1934, 59.
8   Quoted in Gerald Dawe, Notebook, 1991–92, p. 27. Boston College MS 1/8.
9   Gerald Dawe, Typescript, 2. Boston College MS 4/4.
10 Quoted in Chapter 3, 'Northern Windows/Southern Stars', 38.
11 Gerald Dawe, 'The Bright Hour,' *Sunday School* (Oldcastle: Gallery, 1991), 18–19.

Afterword

The futility echoes throughout Dawe's prose collections as he works chambers of allusion and reference that always echo in emptiness.

In a previous world, Patrick Kavanagh complained of his internal estrangement in Dublin from the life that a writer is supposed to lead, of drink, in his case, and a cracked wit, and the life he needs, of quietude, reflection, the original voice. Seamus Heaney diagnosed the parameters of such estrangement in 'Making Strange', realizing that in description we immediately make foreign what has always been familiar, 'reciting … all that I knew, that began to make strange at that same recitation'.[12] James Joyce recognized that dissolution is the end of such imaginative dislocation in 'The Dead', a 'solid world … dissolving and dwindling'.[13]

This sense of fragility, of wasting, of, in the end, mortality, informs Dawe's essays gathered here from that most fragmentary of forms, the literary magazine, the journal, the newspaper, the academic contribution – all gathered with the misleading constancy of an anthology edition, but all significant of change in Dawe's response to the books he reads, and how he reads them. Each piece bears testament to the changing Ireland of the past four decades, as Dawe engages with new revelations of nation and culture as they unfold, with the effect that, in retrospect, we ourselves experience the unsettling sensation that we are forever on the cusp of things, knowing that change has already occurred, but able, for the briefest of moments, to think ourselves back to a time of now remote possibility, to a moment of radical repair where we testify to what might have been:

> Who will ever remember that this was so?
> I can hardly even hear my own footsteps.[14]

A tendency to collect, to list, is long evident in Dawe's work. Here we have Bangor, County Down:

> The boat-houses, the rocky shoreline, the tree filled headland, the lights on the far side of the Lough, the ships and tankers slowly moving in and out of Belfast, the

---

12   Seamus Heaney, 'Making Strange,' *New Selected Poems 1966–1987* (London: Faber, 1997), 154.
13   James Joyce, 'The Dead,' *Dubliners* (New York: Dover, 1991), 152.
14   Gerald Dawe, 'The Journals,' *Irish Times*, 20 March 1993, 9. Boston College MS 2/1.

bustle of men, women and children strolling along the promenade or sitting upon the walls, kids playing 'tig' on the beaches and the unimpressed demeanour of the villas and gardens, Halls and churches....[15]

And here 'Windfall':

> Along the foreshore I take from the sea
> muskets, boxes of butter, timber for housebuilding,
> a lopsided mine, sharks fin, vestments,
> the last landlord's swollen ledger.[16]

This last evokes the beaches of Crete and the west of Ireland, two places at the edge of Europe from which we might look farther abroad. At 'the very core' of Dawe's writing is another list, 'The Old Testament, the legacy of British military history, customs'.[17] It is significant that Dawe's impulse to collect, to create the lasting from the ephemeral, should find home in Greece. Collected amongst Dawe's papers in The Burns Library of Boston College[18] is reference to Acamas, son of Theseus and Phaedra, and companion to Odysseus and his fellow Argives at the siege of Troy. Acamas was one of the brave to infiltrate Troy's walls in the belly of the wooden horse; he was also witness to Odysseus's asphyxiation of Anticlus inside the horse, as Anticlus near cried out in response to Helen, who mimicked the voices of the Greeks' wives in temptation:

> When night came on and sleep held everyone in its grip, the Hellenes from Tenedos sailed near, and Sinon touched the beacon-fire for them at the tomb of Achilles. Meanwhile Helen walked round the horse, calling to the nobles in voices imitative of each one's wife. When Anticlus wanted to reply, Odysseus clamped his mouth shut.[19]

---

15   Gerald Dawe, Notebook, June 1997. Boston College MS 2/4.
16   Gerald Dawe, 'Windfall,' Notebook, 1992–1993. Boston College MS 2/1.
17   Gerald Dawe, 'Finding the Language: The Shankill Speech,' 1 October 1994. Boston College MS 5/4.
18   https://library.bc.edu/finding-aids/MS2000-016-finding-aid.pdf
19   Apollodorus, 'Epitome,' *The Library of Greek Mythology*, trans. K. Aldrich (Coronado: Kansas, 1975), 102.

Acamas experienced that sense of witness and complicity that marks Dawe's writing, that curious combination, typical of a Protestant majority in the north of Ireland that felt the isolation of the Trojan horse, aware of companions' death, in the struggle of a social order secured only by like violence. In this modern drama, Anticlus finds voice, as, escaping Odysseus, he drums the outer shell of the horse, desperate for communication; or, as Dawe figures the reclusive radio enthusiast in 'Atlantic Circle' where

> … the houses mark time,
> slates are in wicked winter realigned,
> and the garbled airwaves
>
> of the ex-Town Clerk radio ham
> plumb across the troubled straits
> finding in his room a dying voice:
> 'This is Ireland calling … this is Ireland …'[20]

The Ireland calling from *Northern Windows/Southern Stars* is quizzical, investigative, self-conscious such as when Dawe suggests that Brendan Kennelly was revolutionary in Ireland because of his identification, and creation, of an audience new (or perhaps reacquainted, as forms of oral recitation are so intrinsic to Irish culture) to poetry, a population previously without voice whose concerns Kennelly, like Paul Durcan, expressed. We can, I think, say the same of Dawe, and connect his work to the development and creation of the Republic under Mary Robinson in the last decade of the twentieth century and that was fundamental to the growth of Ireland as we know it today. In Dawe's prose writings we have that sense of inclusivity, of ethical responsibility, that was the essence of Robinson's project. A sense of worlds passing continues in Dawe's consideration of Yeats as a poet who worked in compensation for a civic society not yet called to being, a preoccupation very much in keeping with the mores of Robinson's republic, with civil rights the new social mantra. There is, in keeping with this growth in self-confidence, an equal growth of self-assertion. Dawe's growing acuity and critique, as the junior anxiety to have everything in right order assumes a questioning, critical voice. In this we

20   Gerald Dawe, 'Atlantic Circle,' *The Lundys Letter* (Dublin: Gallery, 1985), 27.

have a microcosm of Irish writing of the past four decades, of a rising sense of self-worth in society that is alien to the anxious bitterness that Dawe repeatedly, and sadly, identifies in Patrick Kavanagh. Part of this confidence grew from that fact that a writer's entrance to print became easier; Dawe wryly remarks that it was easier to have a poem in print than a job. Equally, self-possession combined with changes in economy and society that so transformed the end of twentieth-century Ireland. What it lacked, amidst the glitter of progress, was an ethics, an answer to how might, as William Carleton put it *The Black Prophet* (1847) in the most desperate of situations, 'the strongest imagery of fiction' transcend 'the terrible realities of Truth?'

Terrible realities are here: mortality, the Troubles, self-sacrifice. But so too are consolations; even Odysseus had a home shore. Sometimes the familiar overwhelms; Dawe's call for a vigorous art is a surrender, in part, to a natural desire for fixity that much of his work opposes. This dual nature, lost, but at home, reminds of the company director who is host to Marlow's monologue in *Heart of Darkness*. The director resembles, Conrad tells us, 'a pilot, which to a seaman is trustworthiness personified'.[21] Dawe's prose inspires a similar confidence. But Conrad's proviso also counts: 'It was difficult to realize' that the director's 'work was not out there in the luminous estuary, but behind him, within the brooding gloom'.[22] Dawe explores his luminous art, in poetry and prose, and through his commentary on the books and writers that attract him; but his real work, as that of the director, is in the brooding gloom, that internal territory where the writer recognizes the geography of his own contradictory impulses. Conrad's scene is the Thames and Congo; so water is a defining motif in Dawe's entire oeuvre, not, as in Yeats's Innisfree, of the lake, but in Dawe, of the sea, of Belfast Lough, Bangor, and beyond. The roadway is there too, the travels across continents, to Australia, Europe, America. The deep heart's core is that solidarity between Dawe's individual probe and the efforts of other writers to understand their situation, the testimony that defies, no matter momentarily, the dissolving world. This then is the meaning of *Northern Windows/Southern Stars*, the due statement, the measured phrase, the

21 Joseph Conrad, *Heart of Darkness* (New York: Dover, 1990), 1.
22 Conrad, *Heart of Darkness*, 1.

construction of which, as re-assembled here, suggests a formal awareness of transitory art (there is savour too in, for example, Tom Paulin's dismissal of Belfast as 'the deep navel of ethnic chutzpah'). From this develops a sense of community that Chekhov would appreciate:

> To lend a helping hand to one's colleague, to respect his personality and labours, not to gossip about him or envy him – to act thus you've got to be not so much the young literary figure as just a plain human being. Let us be ordinary people, let us adopt the same attitude toward all and then an artificially wrought solidarity is not needed.[23]

Dislike of the artificial takes refuge in the irreverent as Dawe remembers elsewhere the opinion of an Irish exile of the 1950s: 'If you were a doctor or even a clerk, you emigrated; we just fucked-off.'[24] Gerald Dawe's deliberations are not set; he is dedicated, after all, to a more fickle god: 'I was not, am not, interested in place. The thing that fascinates me is time.'[25] Poetry, prose, drama, memoir, polemic, history: all confirm to Dawe, in their best moments, a transformation, a brief expression of civility that confirms our social nature and what is often forgotten: that ethics inform aesthetics; due testimony to Dawe's convictions of art and society, 'the passion that cries out of the ordinary'.[26]

[2007–2022]

---

23   Quoted in Gerald Dawe typescript. Boston College MS 4/4.
24   Gerald Dawe, typescript, 'Going places or, the difficulty of staying at home.' Boston College MS 5/3.
25   Gerald Dawe, undated speech. Boston College MS 5/4.
26   Gerald Dawe, 'Sin,' *Sunday school* (Oldcastle: Gallery, 1991), 12.

Bibliography

Aldich, Keith, *The Library of Greek Mythology* (Coronado: Kansas, 1975).
Atwood, Margaret, *Negotiating with the Dead: A Writer on Writing* (Cambridge: Cambridge University Press, 2002).
Bayley, John, *The Uses of Division: Unity and Disharmony in Literature* (London: Chatto & Windus, 1976).
Beckett, Samuel, *Disjecta: Miscellaneous Writings and a Dramatic Fragment* (London: John Calder, 1983).
Bowra, Cecil Maurice, *Politics and Poetry* (Cambridge: Cambridge University Press, 1966).
Boyd, John, *The Middle of My Journey* (Belfast: The Blackstaff Press, 1990).
Brecht, Bertolt, *Bertolt Brecht Poems 1913–1956* (London: Eyre Methuen, 1976).
Brooks, Cleanth, *A Shaping Joy: Studies in the Writer's Craft* (London: Methuen, 1971).
Carleton, William, *The Black Prophet* (London/Belfast: Simms and McIntyre, 1847).
Conrad, Joseph, *Heart of Darkness* (New York: Dover, 1990).
Davie, Donald, *A Gathered Church* (London: Routledge & Kegan Paul, 1978).
Davin, Dan, 'A Memoir', *Collected Poems of W. R. Rodgers* (London: Oxford University Press, 1971).
Dawe, Gerald, 'A Question of Covenants; Modern Irish Poetry', *The Crane Bag*, 3, No. 2 (1979).
——, 'Checkpoints: The Younger Irish Poets', *The Crane Bag*, 6, No. 1 (1982).
——, 'Convention as Conservatism', *The Crane Bag*, 7, No. 2 (1984).
——, 'Poetry and the Public: Solitude and Participation', *The Crane Bag*, 8, No. 2 (1984).
——, 'The Permanent City: The Younger Irish Poets', in *The Irish Writer and the City*, ed. Maurice Harmon (Gerrards Cross: Colin Smythe; Totowa, New Jersey: Barnes & Noble, 1984).
——, *The Lundys Letter* (Dublin: Gallery Press, 1985).
——, *Sunday School* (Oldcastle: Gallery Press, 1991).
——, *The Morning Train* (Oldcastle: Gallery Press, 1999).
——, *The Sound of the Shuttle: Essays on Cultural Belonging & Protestantism in Northern Ireland* (Newbridge: Irish Academic Press, 2020).
Deane, Seamus, 'Synge and Heroism', *Celtic Revivals* (London; Faber and Faber, 1985).
Edwards, Philip, *Threshold of a Nation: A Study in English and Irish Drama* (Cambridge: Cambridge University Press, 1979).

Ellmann, Richard, *Four Dubliners: Wilde, Yeats, Joyce and Beckett* (London: Hamish Hamilton, 1987).
Erlich, Victor, *The Double Image* (Baltimore: Johns Hopkins Press, 1964).
Everett, Barbara, *Poets in Their Time: Essays on English Poets from Donne to Larkin* (London: Faber and Faber, 1986).
Fiacc, Padraic, 'Missa Terribilis: A Sequence', *Paris/Atlantic; An Irish Issue* (American College in Paris, Paris, Summer 1985), subsequently collected in *Missa Terribilis* (Belfast: Blackstaff Press, 1986).
——, *By the Black Stream: Selected Poems 1947–1967* (Dublin: Dolmen Press, 1969).
——, ed., *The Wearing of the Black* (Belfast: The Blackstaff Press, 1974).
——, *Nights in the Bad Place* (Belfast: Blackstaff Press, 1977).
——, *Odour of Blood* (Dublin: The Goldsmith Press, 1973).
——, *Ruined Pages: Selected Poems of Padraic Fiacc*, eds. Gerald Dawe and Aodán Mac Póilin (Belfast: The Blackstaff Press, 1994).
——, *The Selected Padraic Fiacc* (Belfast: Blackstaff Press, 1979).
Gordimer, Nadine, *The Essential Gesture: Writing, Politics and Places* (London: Jonathan Cape, 1988).
Gunn, Thom, *Ben Jonson* (Harmondsworth: Penguin, 1974).
Heaney, Seamus, *Fieldwork* (London: Faber and Faber, 1979).
——, *Preoccupations: Selected Prose* (London: Faber and Faber, 1980).
——, *The Government of the Tongue* (London: Faber and Faber, 1985).
——, *New Selected Poems* (London: Faber and Faber, 1997).
Heine, Heinrich, *Die Bader von Lucca*, in *H. H. Samtliche Werke*, vol. v, ed. Hans Kaufman (Munich: Kindler Verlag, 1964).
Hewitt, John, *Ancestral Voices: The Selected Prose of John Hewitt*, ed. Tom Clyde (Belfast: Blackstaff Press, 1987).
Hoffman, Daniel, *Barbarous Knowledge: Myth in the Poetry of Yeats, Graves and Muir* (London: Oxford University Press, 1970).
Hughes, Robert, 'Who Will Garde the Avant Garde?', *The Irish Times* (23 May 1992).
——, *Nothing If Not Critical* (London: Collins Harvill, 1990).
Joyce, James, *Dubliners* (New York: Dover, 1991).
——, *A Portrait of the Artist as a Young Man* (London: Jonathan Cape, 1920).
Kavanagh, Patrick, 'A Goat Tethered Outside the Bailey', *The Bell* (September 1953).
——, 'Author's Note', *Collected Poems* (London: McGibbon & Kee, 1964).
——, 'I Had a Future', *Selected Poems*, ed. Antoinette Quinn (Harmondsworth, Middlesex: Penguin Books, 1996).
——, *Self-Portrait* (Dublin: The Dolmen Press, 1963).
Kennelly, Brendan, *Breathing Spaces: Early Poems* (Newcastle-upon-Tyne: Bloodaxe Books, 1992).
——, *The Penguin Book of Irish Verse* (Harmondsworth: Penguin Books, 1970).

Kilroy, Thomas, 'The Irish Writer: Self and Society, 1950–80', in *Literature and the Changing Ireland*, ed. Peter Connolly (Bucks: Colin Smythe, 1982).
Kundera, Milan, 'Afterword: A Talk with the Author by Philip Roth', *The Book of Laughter and Forgetting* (Harmondsworth, Middlesex: Penguin Books, 1983).
Larkin, Philip, *Collected Poems* (London: Faber and Faber, 2003).
——, *Required Reading: Miscellaneous Pieces 1955–1982* (London: Faber and Faber, 1983).
Lloyd, David, *Anomalous States: Irish Writing and the Post-Colonial Moment* (Dublin: Lilliput Press, 1993).
Loftus, Richard J. *Nationalism in Modern Anglo-Irish Poetry* (Madison and Milwaukee: University of Wisconsin Press, 1964).
Longley, Edna, *Louis MacNeice: A Study* (London: Faber and Faber, 1988).
Longley, Michael, 'A Neolithic Night: A Note on the Irishness of Louis MacNeice', in *Two Decades of Irish Writing: A Critical Survey,* ed. Douglas Dunn (Cheadle: Carcanet Press, 1975).
——, *Causeway: The Arts in Ulster* (The Arts Council of Northern Ireland with Gill and Macmillan, 1971).
——, 'My Protestant Education', *New Statesman* (10 August 1974).
——, *Poems 1963–1983* (Edinburgh: Salamander Press; Dublin: Gallery Books, 1985).
——, *Tuppeny Stung: Autobiographical Chapters* (Belfast: Lagan Press, 1994).
Lowell, Robert, *Collected Prose* (London: Faber and Faber, 1987).
Lucy, Sean, *Unfinished Sequence* (Dublin: Wolfhound Press, 1979).
MacNeice, Louis, *Modern Poetry*: *A Personal Essay* (Oxford: Oxford University Press, 1938).
——, *Selected Literary Criticism of Louis MacNeice*, ed. Alan Heuser (Oxford: Clarendon Press, 1987).
——, *The Collected Poems of Louis MacNeice*, ed. Eric Robertson Dodds (London: Faber & Faber, 1979).
——, *The Poetry of W. B. Yeats* (London: Faber and Faber, 1941).
——, *The Strings Are False* (London: Faber and Faber, 1965).
——, *Varieties of Parable* (Cambridge: Cambridge University Press, 1965).
Mahon, Derek, *Poems 1962–1978* (London: Oxford University Press, 1979).
——, *Journalism: Selected Prose 1970–1995* (Oldcastle: Gallery Press, 1996).
——, *The Hunt by Night* (Oxford: Oxford University Press, 1982).
Mandelstam, Osip, *The Complete Critical Prose and Letters*, ed. J. G. Harris (Ann Arbor, MI: Ardis, 1979).
Massie, Allan, *The Death of Men* (London: The Bodley Head, 1981).
McGahern, John, *High Ground* (London: Faber and Faber, 1985).
Milosz, Czeslaw, *The Captive Mind* (Harmondsworth, Middlesex: Penguin Books, 1980).

Montague, John, 'Regionalism into Reconciliation: The Poetry of John Hewitt', *The Figure in the Cave and Other Essays* (Dublin: Lilliput, 1989).
——, *A Chosen Light* (London: MacGibbon and Kee, 1967).
——, *A Slow Dance* (Dublin: Dolmen Press, 1975).
——, ed., *The Faber Book of Irish Verse* (London: Faber, 1974).
——, *Selected Poems* (London: Oxford University Press, 1982) and *New Selected Poems* (Meath: The Gallery Press, 1989).
——, *The Dead Kingdom* (Belfast: Blackstaff Press; Dublin: Dolmen Press, 1984).
——, *The Great Cloak* (Dublin: Dolmen Press, 1978).
——, *The Rough Field* (Meath: The Gallery Press, 1989).
Montale, Eugenio, *The Second Life of Art: Selected Essays* (New York: The Ecco Press, 1982).
Morrison, Blake; Motion, Andrew, eds., Introduction to *The Penguin Book of Contemporary British Poetry* (London: Penguin Books, 1982).
Murray, Les, *The Peasant Mandarin* (Queensland: University of Queensland Press, 1978).
Nelson, Sarah, *Ulster's Uncertain Defenders: Loyalists and the Northern Ireland Conflict* (Belfast: Appletree Press, 1984).
O'Connor, Flannery, 'Writing Short Stories', *Mystery and Manners: Occasional Prose* (London: Faber and Faber, 1972).
O'Driscoll, Dennis, 'Irish Roundup', *Poetry Review*, 79, No. 1 (1989).
O'Faoláin, Seán, *The Irish* (Harmondsworth, Middlesex: Penguin Books, 1969).
Ormsby, Frank, ed., *A Rage for Order: Poetry of the Northern Ireland Troubles* (Belfast: The Blackstaff Press, 1992).
——, *Poets from the North of Ireland* (Belfast: The Blackstaff Press, 1979; 2nd ed. 1990).
——, *Northern Windows* (Belfast: Blackstaff Press, 1987).
Paulin, Tom, *A State of Justice* (London: Faber and Faber, 1977).
——, *Ireland and the English Crisis* (Newcastle upon Tyne: Bloodaxe Books, 1984).
——, *Liberty Tree* (London: Faber and Faber, 1983).
——, *The Strange Museum* (London: Faber and Faber, 1980).
——, *Writing to the Moment: Selected Critical Essays 1980–1996* (London: Faber and Faber, 1996).
——, *Fivemiletown* (London: Faber and Faber, 1987).
——, *The Faber Book of Political Verse*, ed. Tom Paulin (London: Faber and Faber, 1986).
Porter, Peter, 'Privileges of an Irish Poet,' *The Sunday Telegraph* (30 August 1998).
Pound, Ezra, 'John Synge and the Habits of Criticism', *Egoist*, 1:3 (2 February 1914).
——, *ABC of Reading* (London: Faber and Faber, 1951).

Quinn, Antoinette, 'The Well-Beloved: Montague and the Muse', *Irish University Review*, 19, No. 1 (Spring, 1989).
Rodgers, W. R., *Poems,* ed. Michael Longley (Oldcastle: The Gallery Press, 1993).
Ryan, John, *Remembering How We Stood* (Mullingar: Lilliput Press, 1987 [orig. ed. 1975]).
Said, Edward W., *The World, the Text, and the Critic* (London: Faber and Faber, 1984).
Skelton, Robin, *J. M. Synge: Collected Works, Vol. I., Poems* (London: Oxford University Press, 1962).
Smith, Iain Crichton, *Towards the Human: Selected Essays* (Edinburgh: Macdonald, 1986).
Spender, Stephen, *Love-Hate Relations: A Study of Anglo-American Sensibilities* (London: Hamish Hamilton, 1974).
Stanford, William Bedell, *Enemies of Poetry* (London: Routledge & Kegan Paul, 1980).
Williams, Raymond, *Politics and Letters: Interviews with New Left Review* (London: N.L.B. Verso ed., 1981).
——, *The Country and the City* (London: Paladin, 1975).
Yeats, W. B., 'J. M. Synge and the Ireland of His Time', *Essays and Introductions* (New York: Macmillan, 1961).
——, *Yeats's Poems,* ed. A. Norman Jeffares (Basingstoke: Palgrave, 1996).

Reimagining Ireland

Series Editor: Dr Eamon Maher, Technological University Dublin

The concepts of Ireland and 'Irishness' are in constant flux in the wake of an ever-increasing reappraisal of the notion of cultural and national specificity in a world assailed from all angles by the forces of globalisation and uniformity. Reimagining Ireland interrogates Ireland's past and present and suggests possibilities for the future by looking at Ireland's literature, culture and history and subjecting them to the most up-to-date critical appraisals associated with sociology, literary theory, historiography, political science and theology.

Some of the pertinent issues include, but are not confined to, Irish writing in English and Irish, Nationalism, Unionism, the Northern 'Troubles', the Peace Process, economic development in Ireland, the impact and decline of the Celtic Tiger, Irish spirituality, the rise and fall of organised religion, the visual arts, popular cultures, sport, Irish music and dance, emigration and the Irish diaspora, immigration and multiculturalism, marginalisation, globalisation, modernity/postmodernity and postcolonialism. The series publishes monographs, comparative studies, interdisciplinary projects, conference proceedings and edited books. Proposals should be sent either to Dr Eamon Maher at eamon.maher@ittdublin.ie or to ireland@peterlang.com.

Vol. 1	Eugene O'Brien: 'Kicking Bishop Brennan up the Arse': Negotiating Texts and Contexts in Contemporary Irish Studies ISBN 978-3-03911-539-6. 219 pages. 2009.
Vol. 2	James P.Byrne, Padraig Kirwan and Michael O'Sullivan (eds): Affecting Irishness: Negotiating Cultural Identity Within and Beyond the Nation ISBN 978-3-03911-830-4. 334 pages. 2009.
Vol. 3	Irene Lucchitti: The Islandman: The Hidden Life of Tomás O'Crohan ISBN 978-3-03911-837-3. 232 pages. 2009.
Vol. 4	Paddy Lyons and Alison O'Malley-Younger (eds): No Country for Old Men: Fresh Perspectives on Irish Literature ISBN 978-3-03911-841-0. 289 pages. 2009.

| Vol. 5 | Eamon Maher (ed.): Cultural Perspectives on Globalisation and Ireland
ISBN 978-3-03911-851-9. 256 pages. 2009. |
|---|---|
| Vol. 6 | Lynn Brunet: 'A Course of Severe and Arduous Trials': Bacon, Beckett and Spurious Freemasonry in Early Twentieth-Century Ireland
ISBN 978-3-03911-854-0. 218 pages. 2009. |
| Vol. 7 | Claire Lynch: Irish Autobiography: Stories of Self in the Narrative of a Nation
ISBN 978-3-03911-856-4. 234 pages. 2009. |
| Vol. 8 | Victoria O'Brien: A History of Irish Ballet from 1927 to 1963
ISBN 978-3-03911-873-1. 208 pages. 2011. |
| Vol. 9 | Irene Gilsenan Nordin and Elin Holmsten (eds): Liminal Borderlands in Irish Literature and Culture
ISBN 978-3-03911-859-5. 208 pages. 2009. |
| Vol. 10 | Claire Nally: Envisioning Ireland: W. B. Yeats's Occult Nationalism
ISBN 978-3-03911-882-3. 320 pages. 2010. |
| Vol. 11 | Raita Merivirta: The Gun and Irish Politics: Examining National History in Neil Jordan's *Michael Collins*
ISBN 978-3-03911-888-5. 202 pages. 2009. |
| Vol. 12 | John Strachan and Alison O'Malley-Younger (eds): Ireland: Revolution and Evolution
ISBN 978-3-03911-881-6. 248 pages. 2010. |
| Vol. 13 | Barbara Hughes: Between Literature and History: The Diaries and Memoirs of Mary Leadbeater and Dorothea Herbert
ISBN 978-3-03911-889-2. 255 pages. 2010. |
| Vol. 14 | Edwina Keown and Carol Taaffe (eds): Irish Modernism: Origins, Contexts, Publics
ISBN 978-3-03911-894-6. 256 pages. 2010. |
| Vol. 15 | John Walsh: Contests and Contexts: The Irish Language and Ireland's Socio-Economic Development
ISBN 978-3-03911-914-1. 492 pages. 2011. |

Vol. 16   Zélie Asava: The Black Irish Onscreen: Representing Black and Mixed-Race Identities on Irish Film and Television
ISBN 978-3-0343-0839-7. 213 pages. 2013.

Vol. 17   Susan Cahill and Eóin Flannery (eds): This Side of Brightness: Essays on the Fiction of Colum McCann
ISBN 978-3-03911-935-6. 189 pages. 2012.

Vol. 18   Brian Arkins: The Thought of W. B. Yeats
ISBN 978-3-03911-939-4. 204 pages. 2010.

Vol. 19   Maureen O'Connor: The Female and the Species: The Animal in Irish Women's Writing
ISBN 978-3-03911-959-2. 203 pages. 2010.

Vol. 20   Rhona Trench: Bloody Living: The Loss of Selfhood in the Plays of Marina Carr
ISBN 978-3-03911-964-6. 327 pages. 2010.

Vol. 21   Jeannine Woods: Visions of Empire and Other Imaginings: Cinema, Ireland and India, 1910–1962
ISBN 978-3-03911-974-5. 230 pages. 2011.

Vol. 22   Neil O'Boyle: New Vocabularies, Old Ideas: Culture, Irishness and the Advertising Industry
ISBN 978-3-03911-978-3. 233 pages. 2011.

Vol. 23   Dermot McCarthy: John McGahern and the Art of Memory
ISBN 978-3-0343-0100-8. 344 pages. 2010.

Vol. 24   Francesca Benatti, Sean Ryder and Justin Tonra (eds): Thomas Moore: Texts, Contexts, Hypertexts
ISBN 978-3-0343-0900-4. 220 pages. 2013.

Vol. 25   Sarah O'Connor: No Man's Land: Irish Women and the Cultural Present
ISBN 978-3-0343-0111-4. 230 pages. 2011.

Vol. 26   Caroline Magennis: Sons of Ulster: Masculinities in the Contemporary Northern Irish Novel
ISBN 978-3-0343-0110-7. 192 pages. 2010.

Vol. 27   Dawn Duncan: Irish Myth, Lore and Legend on Film
           ISBN 978-3-0343-0140-4. 181 pages. 2013.

Vol. 28   Eamon Maher and Catherine Maignant (eds): Franco-Irish
           Connections in Space and Time: Peregrinations and Ruminations
           ISBN 978-3-0343-0870-0. 295 pages. 2012.

Vol. 29   Holly Maples: Culture War: Conflict, Commemoration and the
           Contemporary Abbey Theatre
           ISBN 978-3-0343-0137-4. 294 pages. 2011.

Vol. 30   Maureen O'Connor (ed.): Back to the Future of Irish
           Studies: Festschrift for Tadhg Foley
           ISBN 978-3-0343-0141-1. 359 pages. 2010.

Vol. 31   Eva Urban: Community Politics and the Peace Process in
           Contemporary Northern Irish Drama
           ISBN 978-3-0343-0143-5. 303 pages. 2011.

Vol. 32   Mairéad Conneely: Between Two Shores/*Idir Dhá Chladach*: Writing
           the Aran Islands, 1890–1980
           ISBN 978-3-0343-0144-2. 299 pages. 2011.

Vol. 33   Gerald Morgan and Gavin Hughes (eds): Southern Ireland and the
           Liberation of France: New Perspectives
           ISBN 978-3-0343-0190-9. 250 pages. 2011.

Vol. 34   Anne MacCarthy: Definitions of Irishness in the 'Library of
           Ireland' Literary Anthologies
           ISBN 978-3-0343-0194-7. 271 pages. 2012.

Vol. 35   Irene Lucchitti: Peig Sayers: In Her Own Write
           ISBN 978-3-0343-0253-1. Forthcoming.

Vol. 36   Eamon Maher and Eugene O'Brien (eds): Breaking the
           Mould: Literary Representations of Irish Catholicism
           ISBN 978-3-0343-0232-6. 249 pages. 2011.

Vol. 37   Mícheál Ó hAodha and John O'Callaghan (eds): Narratives of the
           Occluded Irish Diaspora: Subversive Voices
           ISBN 978-3-0343-0248-7. 227 pages. 2012.

Vol. 38   Willy Maley and Alison O'Malley-Younger (eds): Celtic Connections: Irish–Scottish Relations and the Politics of Culture
ISBN 978-3-0343-0214-2. 247 pages. 2013.

Vol. 39   Sabine Egger and John McDonagh (eds): Polish–Irish Encounters in the Old and New Europe
ISBN 978-3-0343-0253-1. 322 pages. 2011.

Vol. 40   Elke D'hoker, Raphaël Ingelbien and Hedwig Schwall (eds): Irish Women Writers: New Critical Perspectives
ISBN 978-3-0343-0249-4. 318 pages. 2011.

Vol. 41   Peter James Harris: From Stage to Page: Critical Reception of Irish Plays in the London Theatre, 1925–1996
ISBN 978-3-0343-0266-1. 311 pages. 2011.

Vol. 42   Hedda Friberg-Harnesk, Gerald Porter and Joakim Wrethed (eds): Beyond Ireland: Encounters Across Cultures
ISBN 978-3-0343-0270-8. 342 pages. 2011.

Vol. 43   Irene Gilsenan Nordin and Carmen Zamorano Llena (eds): Urban and Rural Landscapes in Modern Ireland: Language, Literature and Culture
ISBN 978-3-0343-0279-1. 238 pages. 2012.

Vol. 44   Kathleen Costello-Sullivan: Mother/Country: Politics of the Personal in the Fiction of Colm Tóibín
ISBN 978-3-0343-0753-6. 247 pages. 2012.

Vol. 45   Lesley Lelourec and Gráinne O'Keeffe-Vigneron (eds): Ireland and Victims: Confronting the Past, Forging the Future
ISBN 978-3-0343-0792-5. 331 pages. 2012.

Vol. 46   Gerald Dawe, Darryl Jones and Nora Pelizzari (eds): Beautiful Strangers: Ireland and the World of the 1950s
ISBN 978-3-0343-0801-4. 207 pages. 2013.

Vol. 47   Yvonne O'Keeffe and Claudia Reese (eds): New Voices, Inherited Lines: Literary and Cultural Representations of the Irish Family
ISBN 978-3-0343-0799-4. 238 pages. 2013.

Vol. 48	Justin Carville (ed.): Visualizing Dublin: Visual Culture, Modernity and the Representation of Urban Space ISBN 978-3-0343-0802-1. 326 pages. 2014.
Vol. 49	Gerald Power and Ondřej Pilný (eds): Ireland and the Czech Lands: Contacts and Comparisons in History and Culture ISBN 978-3-0343-1701-6. 243 pages. 2014.
Vol. 50	Eoghan Smith: John Banville: Art and Authenticity ISBN 978-3-0343-0852-6. 199 pages. 2014.
Vol. 51	María Elena Jaime de Pablos and Mary Pierse (eds): George Moore and the Quirks of Human Nature ISBN 978-3-0343-1752-8. 283 pages. 2014.
Vol. 52	Aidan O'Malley and Eve Patten (eds): Ireland, West to East: Irish Cultural Connections with Central and Eastern Europe ISBN 978-3-0343-0913-4. 307 pages. 2014.
Vol. 53	Ruben Moi, Brynhildur Boyce and Charles I. Armstrong (eds): The Crossings of Art in Ireland ISBN 978-3-0343-0983-7. 319 pages. 2014.
Vol. 54	Sylvie Mikowski (ed.): Ireland and Popular Culture ISBN 978-3-0343-1717-7. 257 pages. 2014.
Vol. 55	Benjamin Keatinge and Mary Pierse (eds): France and Ireland in the Public Imagination ISBN 978-3-0343-1747-4. 279 pages. 2014.
Vol. 56	Raymond Mullen, Adam Bargroff and Jennifer Mullen (eds): John McGahern: Critical Essays ISBN 978-3-0343-1755-9. 253 pages. 2014.
Vol. 57	Máirtín Mac Con Iomaire and Eamon Maher (eds): 'Tickling the Palate': Gastronomy in Irish Literature and Culture ISBN 978-3-0343-1769-6. 253 pages. 2014.
Vol. 58	Heidi Hansson and James H. Murphy (eds): Fictions of the Irish Land War ISBN 978-3-0343-0999-8. 237 pages. 2014.

Vol. 59 Fiona McCann: A Poetics of Dissensus: Confronting Violence in Contemporary Prose Writing from the North of Ireland
ISBN 978-3-0343-0979-0. 238 pages. 2014.

Vol. 60 Marguérite Corporaal, Christopher Cusack, Lindsay Janssen and Ruud van den Beuken (eds): Global Legacies of the Great Irish Famine: Transnational and Interdisciplinary Perspectives
ISBN 978-3-0343-0903-5. 357 pages. 2014.

Vol. 61 Katarzyna Ojrzyn'ska: 'Dancing As If Language No Longer Existed': Dance in Contemporary Irish Drama
ISBN 978-3-0343-1813-6. 318 pages. 2015.

Vol. 62 Whitney Standlee: 'Power to Observe': Irish Women Novelists in Britain, 1890–1916
ISBN 978-3-0343-1837-2. 288 pages. 2015.

Vol. 63 Elke D'hoker and Stephanie Eggermont (eds): The Irish Short Story: Traditions and Trends
ISBN 978-3-0343-1753-5. 330 pages. 2015.

Vol. 64 Radvan Markus: Echoes of the Rebellion: The Year 1798 in Twentieth-Century Irish Fiction and Drama
ISBN 978-3-0343-1832-7. 248 pages. 2015.

Vol. 65 B. Mairéad Pratschke: Visions of Ireland: Gael Linn's *Amharc Éireann* Film Series, 1956–1964
ISBN 978-3-0343-1872-3. 301 pages. 2015.

Vol. 66 Una Hunt and Mary Pierse (eds): France and Ireland: Notes and Narratives
ISBN 978-3-0343-1914-0. 272 pages. 2015.

Vol. 67 John Lynch and Katherina Dodou (eds): The Leaving of Ireland: Migration and Belonging in Irish Literature and Film
ISBN 978-3-0343-1896-9. 313 pages. 2015.

Vol. 68 Anne Goarzin (ed.): New Critical Perspectives on Franco-Irish Relations
ISBN 978-3-0343-1781-8. 271 pages. 2015.

| Vol. 69 | Michel Brunet, Fabienne Gaspari and Mary Pierse (eds): George Moore's Paris and His Ongoing French Connections
ISBN 978-3-0343-1973-7. 279 pages. 2015. |

| Vol. 70 | Carine Berbéri and Martine Pelletier (eds): Ireland: Authority and Crisis
ISBN 978-3-0343-1939-3. 296 pages. 2015. |

| Vol. 71 | David Doolin: Transnational Revolutionaries: The Fenian Invasion of Canada, 1866
ISBN 978-3-0343-1922-5. 348 pages. 2016. |

| Vol. 72 | Terry Phillips: Irish Literature and the First World War: Culture, Identity and Memory
ISBN 978-3-0343-1969-0. 297 pages. 2015. |

| Vol. 73 | Carmen Zamorano Llena and Billy Gray (eds): Authority and Wisdom in the New Ireland: Studies in Literature and Culture
ISBN 978-3-0343-1833-4. 263 pages. 2016. |

| Vol. 74 | Flore Coulouma (ed.): New Perspectives on Irish TV Series: Identity and Nostalgia on the Small Screen
ISBN 978-3-0343-1977-5. 222 pages. 2016. |

| Vol. 75 | Fergal Lenehan: Stereotypes, Ideology and Foreign Correspondents: German Media Representations of Ireland, 1946–2010
ISBN 978-3-0343-2222-5. 306 pages. 2016. |

| Vol. 76 | Jarlath Killeen and Valeria Cavalli (eds): 'Inspiring a Mysterious Terror': 200 Years of Joseph Sheridan Le Fanu
ISBN 978-3-0343-2223-2. 260 pages. 2016. |

| Vol. 77 | Anne Karhio: 'Slight Return': Paul Muldoon's Poetics of Place
ISBN 978-3-0343-1986-7. 272 pages. 2017. |

| Vol. 78 | Margaret Eaton: Frank Confessions: Performance in the Life-Writings of Frank McCourt
ISBN 978-1-906165-61-1. 294 pages. 2017. |

Vol. 79   Marguérite Corporaal, Christopher Cusack and Ruud van den Beuken (eds): Irish Studies and the Dynamics of Memory: Transitions and Transformations
ISBN 978-3-0343-2236-2. 360 pages. 2017.

Vol. 80   Conor Caldwell and Eamon Byers (eds): New Crops, Old Fields: Reimagining Irish Folklore
ISBN 978-3-0343-1912-6. 200 pages. 2017.

Vol. 81   Sinéad Wall: Irish Diasporic Narratives in Argentina: A Reconsideration of Home, Identity and Belonging
ISBN 978-1-906165-66-6. 282 pages. 2017.

Vol. 82   Ute Anna Mittermaier: Images of Spain in Irish Literature, 1922–1975
ISBN 978-3-0343-1993-5. 386 pages. 2017.

Vol. 83   Lauren Clark: Consuming Irish Children: Advertising and the Art of Independence, 1860–1921
ISBN 978-3-0343-1989-8. 288 pages. 2017.

Vol. 84   Lisa FitzGerald: Re-Place: Irish Theatre Environments
ISBN 978-1-78707-359-3. 222 pages. 2017.

Vol. 85   Joseph Greenwood: 'Hear My Song': Irish Theatre and Popular Song in the 1950s and 1960s
ISBN 978-3-0343-1915-7. 320 pages. 2017.

Vol. 86   Nils Beese: Writing Slums: Dublin, Dirt and Literature
ISBN 978-1-78707-959-5. 250 pages. 2018.

Vol. 87   Barry Houlihan (ed.): Navigating Ireland's Theatre Archive: Theory, Practice, Performance
ISBN 978-1-78707-372-2. 306 pages. 2019.

Vol. 88   María Elena Jaime de Pablos (ed.): Giving Shape to the Moment: The Art of Mary O'Donnell: Poet, Novelist and Short Story Writer
ISBN 978-1-78874-403-4. 228 pages. 2018.

Vol. 89	Marguérite Corporaal and Peter Gray (eds): The Great Irish Famine and Social Class: Conflicts, Responsibilities, Representations ISBN 978-1-78874-166-8. 330 pages. 2019.
Vol. 90	Patrick Speight: Irish-Argentine Identity in an Age of Political Challenge and Change, 1875–1983 ISBN 978-1-78874-417-1. 360 pages. 2020.
Vol. 91	Fionna Barber, Heidi Hansson, and Sara Dybris McQuaid (eds): Ireland and the North ISBN 978-1-78874-289-4. 338 pages. 2019.
Vol. 92	Ruth Sheehy: The Life and Work of Richard King: Religion, Nationalism and Modernism ISBN 978-1-78707-246-6. 482 pages. 2019.
Vol. 93	Brian Lucey, Eamon Maher and Eugene O'Brien (eds): Recalling the Celtic Tiger ISBN 978-1-78997-286-3. 386 pages. 2019.
Vol. 94	Melania Terrazas Gallego (ed.): Trauma and Identity in Contemporary Irish Culture ISBN 978-1-78997-557-4. 302 pages. 2020.
Vol. 95	Patricia Medcalf: Advertising the Black Stuff in Ireland 1959–1999: Increments of Change ISBN 978-1-78997-345-7. 218 pages. 2020.
Vol. 96	Anne Goarzin and Maria Parsons (eds): New Cartographies, Nomadic Methologies: Contemporary Arts, Culture and Politics in Ireland ISBN 978-1-78874-651-9. 204 pages. 2020.
Vol. 97	Hiroko Ikeda and Kazuo Yokouchi (eds): Irish Literature in the British Context and Beyond: New Perspectives from Kyoto ISBN 978-1-78997-566-6. 250 pages. 2020.
Vol. 98	Catherine Nealy Judd: Travel Narratives of the Irish Famine: Politics, Tourism, and Scandal, 1845–1853 ISBN 978-1-80079-084-1. 468 pages. 2020.

Vol. 99	Lesley Lelourec and Gráinne O'Keeffe-Vigneron (eds): Northern Ireland after the Good Friday Agreement: Building a Shared Future from a Troubled Past? ISBN 978-1-78997-746-2. 262 pages. 2021.
Vol. 100	Eamon Maher and Eugene O'Brien (eds): Reimagining Irish Studies for the Twenty-First Century ISBN 978-1-80079-191-6. 384 pages. 2021.
Vol. 101	Nathalie Sebbane: Memorialising the Magdalene Laundries: From Story to History ISBN 978-1-78707-589-4. 334 pages. 2021.
Vol 102	Roz Goldie: A Dangerous Pursuit: The Anti-Sectarian Work of Counteract ISBN 978-1-80079-187-9. 268 pages. 2021.
Vol. 103	Ann Wilson: The Picture Postcard: A New Window into Edwardian Ireland ISBN 978-1-78874-079-1. 282 pages. 2021.
Vol. 104	Anna Charczun: Irish Lesbian Writing Across Time: A New Framework for Rethinking Love Between Women ISBN 978-1-78997-864-3. 320 pages. 2022.
Vol. 105	Olivier Coquelin, Brigitte Bastiat and Frank Healy (eds): Northern Ireland: Challenges of Peace and Reconciliation Since the Good Friday Agreement ISBN 978-1-78997-817-9. 298 pages. 2022.
Vol. 106	Jo Murphy-Lawless and Laury Oaks (eds): The Salley Gardens: Women, Sex, and Motherhood in Ireland ISBN 978-1-80079-417-7. 338 pages. 2022.
Vol. 107	Mercedes del Campo: Voices from the Margins: Gender and the Everyday in Women's Pre- and Post-Agreement Troubles Short Fiction ISBN 978-1-78874-330-3. 324 pages. 2022.
Vol. 108	Sean McGraw and Jonathan Tiernan: The Politics of Irish Primary Education: Reform in an Era of Secularisation ISBN 978-1-80079-709-3. Forthcoming. 2022.

Vol. 109 Gerald Dawe: Northern Windows/Southern Stars: Selected Early Essays 1983–1994
ISBN 978-1-80079-652-2. 180 pages. 2022.

www.ingramcontent.com/pod-product-compliance
Ingram Content Group UK Ltd.
Pitfield, Milton Keynes, MK11 3LW, UK
UKHW021311180426
11947UKWH00015B/1166